Books by Richard Rhodes

FICTION

Sons of Earth
The Last Safari
Holy Secrets
The Ungodly

VERITY

A Hole in the World
Farm
The Making of the Atomic Bomb
Looking for America
The Inland Ground

MAKING LOVE

An Erotic Odyssey

Richard Rhodes

SIMON & SCHUSTER
New York London Toronto Sydney Tokyo Singapore

SIMON & SCHUSTER
Simon & Schuster Building
Rockefeller Center
1230 Avenue of the Americas
New York, New York 10020

SIMON & SCHUSTER and colophon are registered trademarks
of Simon & Schuster Inc.

Designed by Levavi & Levavi
Manufactured in the United States of America

1   3   5   7   9   10   8   6   4   2

Library of Congress Cataloging in Publication Data

Rhodes, Richard.
Making love: an erotic odyssey/Richard Rhodes.
p.   cm.
1. Men—United States—Sexual behavior—Case studies.   2. Rhodes,
Richard.   I. Title.
HQ28.R48 1992
306.7'081—dc20   92-12467
                                                                CIP
ISBN: 0-671-78227-4

*"Brown Penny" by W. B. Yeats. Reprinted with permission of Mac-
millan Publishing Company from* The Poems of W. B. Yeats: A New
Edition, *edited by Richard J. Finneran (New York: Macmillan, 1983).*

For
Polly Valley
and
Willie T. Longmeyer

Contents

Generally the reader wants his narrator to be upright, decent, honest, and not prone to the lusts that plague other people— never ourselves.

—D. M. Thomas, *Lying Together*

We are all made up of fragments, so shapelessly and strangely assembled that every moment, every piece plays its own game. And there is as much difference between us and ourselves as between us and others.

—Montaigne, *Essays*

Preface

There are war stories and tales of survival, there are political memoirs and confessions of faith, but in all of Western literature there are only a very few personal narratives that honestly and frankly explore the intimate experience of making love—and hardly any to which an author has been willing to sign his name. Although sex is one of the perplexing, joyous, difficult and transcendent experiences of life, although studies indicate that people think about sex dozens of times every living day, hardly anyone has come forward to write about it intimately except behind the mask of fiction. Fiction is fine, but using fiction as a disguise makes both the uniqueness of intimate experience and its common humanity easy to dispute. *Making Love* is fact: "verity," as I call nonfiction. It happened. Everything in this book is true.

Why talk about it? People asked that question angrily when Alfred Kinsey published his reports of male and female sexual behavior. They asked it again when William Masters and Virginia Johnson described human sexual response from laboratory observation. The question implies that sexuality is better left unreported and unexamined.

Any number of angry newspaper editorialists, psychiatrists and other self-appointed guardians of public morality in the days of Kinsey and Masters and Johnson argued just that. They claimed that studying how people make love, observing it, examining it was misguided and even immoral. They complained that doing so would take away the romance. Romance is alive and well all these years later and there's marginally less sexual dysfunction than there used to be, so I'm told. Sex is a skill like any other, whether or not it's informed and deepened by love; why shouldn't we learn what other people have made of it?

But who am *I* then to talk about it? Alfred Kinsey was an entomologist, the world's leading and perhaps only expert on the gall wasp (I've seen his collection of several million specimens at Harvard's Museum of Comparative Zoology). William Masters is an obstetrician and gynecologist. Virginia Johnson trained as a singer. I'm a writer. Emerson said something self-revealing once about the kind of person who writes: "[The writer] counts it all nonsense, that they say, that some things are indescribable. He believes that all that can be thought can be written, first or last; and he would report the Holy Ghost, or attempt it." I do believe that, and more: I believe that all that can be thought *must* be spoken and written, communicated and shared, that ignorance and silence are pain, that to speak (to write) is to contribute to alleviating that pain.

Making Love follows from my previous book *A Hole in the World.* I traveled across the country discussing *A Hole in the World.* Everywhere I went, people took me aside—media people, tour escorts, people in the audience, fellow passengers on airplanes—to confess to me their own painful experiences of child abuse. In many cases my speaking out allowed them to speak out. I began to wonder if people who were abused as children don't in fact constitute a majority in the United States (if you count physical punishment as abuse, which it is, they do). Back home I found the first deliveries of hundreds of letters from people reporting their experiences of abuse, many of those experiences far more terrible than mine. Letters still arrive at the rate of five or ten a week. I answer them all. People are grateful that someone was willing to explore honestly and publicly his personal experiences of mistreatment. No one has yet complained in my hearing that child abuse is better off unexplored and unexamined, that writing about it ruins the family romance.

Yet I knew when I wrote *A Hole in the World* that I had left out crucial episodes and crucial lessons. Some of my experience I hadn't yet fully understood. Some I wasn't ready to talk about publicly.

I've come to realize that I survived my stepmother's brutal abuse partly because I was a bright, attractive child who liked to read and found favor with teachers at school. I had the good luck to be helped along the way—by my beloved brother Stanley most of all—and then to be rescued.

But I also survived, in the years after my rescue and well into adulthood, by using my sexuality to structure and confine the extensive psychological damage the years of abuse had inflicted on me. That is, I worked my way through that damage not only with my mind but also with my body. How could it be otherwise when mind and body are one? Abuse is written on the body as well as on the soul. (Fortunately, so is the abundance of our common humanity; so is love. Who has never felt the offering of another person's body as a gift of grace?) And however unfit for the parlor, such survival skills ought to be shared. The taboo against writing about one's personal sexual experience cuts us off from valuable knowledge. In *Making Love* I share what I learned. You may or may not find the experience comfortable. "The loves of flint and iron"—Emerson again—"are naturally a little rougher than those of the nightingale and the rose."

Writing about my experiences of intimacy required solving a technical problem that enclosed an ethical question. To protect my partners' privacy I had, paradoxically, to reveal *only* their privacy, to leave out everything that would identify them publicly. On first inspection that may make my focus seem pathological, my relationships ghostly and my partners ghosts of the flesh. The alternative would have been to invent public identities for my partners, but to do that would have been to launch the book into fiction. So I say again: what follows isn't fiction, it's verity. I think you will find imagining public identities for my partners as problematic as you would find it problematic to visualize them physically having only heard their voices. That in itself says something important about how divided we are—as divided as the citizens of authoritarian regimes who keep their thoughts of freedom to themselves, even from their families; as divided as the explosive murderers of whom the neighbors say they were quiet and good.

Ethically, it seems to me I violate no more privacy by sharing the experiences I shared than clinicians do who report on their encounters with unnamed patients. We value such reports even though not all patients, however protected, are likely to be comfortable with their publication. I hope what I've reported is similarly valuable. With one obvious exception, the initials I use to designate individuals bear no relationship to their real names.

Sex is a sovereignty waiting to be explored, just as consciousness was for early modern fiction. I'm a writer. Writing is my work. Painters may paint their real lovers realistically, even their lovers making love, without scandal except among the philistines. Why shouldn't writers do likewise? "Write about what you know." I have. Good luck with it.

The body against death and all terror.

I Lost My
Virginity . . .

I lost my virginity to a New York dance-hall girl when I was eighteen. I use the words "virginity" and "girl" in their conventional senses. Of the many virginities forfeit across a lifetime, I had already given up two, and the girl was a muscular woman, hard-faced but kind, a part-time prostitute at least forty years old.

I'd spent my adolescence at a boys' home and farm in Independence, Missouri. I was skinny and morbidly shy when I arrived at Yale on scholarship in 1955—all pecker and feet, as Ozark people say. By the next spring, lonely, seeing my classmates dating, blind-dating myself but barely able to muster enough presence to kiss a date goodnight, I was desperate. I told a fellow freshman, H——, my problem. I'm not sure why I told him; I'd hardly spoken to him outside of class before. He was private school Greek-American—a classic nose, a head of curly hair, cocky, literal-minded, not all that bright. I suppose I thought he knew his way around.

If only I could get past my wearisome virginity, I told H——, maybe I wouldn't be so shy with a date. I'd have more confidence. I'd know what to do.

H—— knew what to do. He'd heard about two sisters in New York, he said, who were notorious for relieving geek preppies and weeny Yalies of their virginity, the King sisters, Gussie and Sally, dance-hall girls. If I was serious, he'd find out how to get in touch with them. He'd take me down to New York and they'd fix me up. It would probably cost some money. Maybe forty bucks. Was I serious? I was serious. He'd see what he could do.

Across the weekend and into the next week, coming and going to class, studying in my room, I thought about H——'s plan, fantasized about it, but I didn't really believe it. It was like signing on for a parachute jump: easy to do because you can't imagine ever actually jumping out of a plane. But later in the week H—— called me and said he'd talked to one of the sisters and we were on. My heart started pounding. I was avid. I was also terrified.

We took a Saturday morning train to Grand Central and then a taxi. Somewhere in Brooklyn or Queens. We found the block but couldn't find the address. H—— called from a pay phone on the corner. The doorway next to the Tammany Hall mid-block, a second-floor apartment, up a flight of stairs.

The older sister answered the door, Gussie, a great head of bleached hair and a tough face swollen with smoking and booze. I still hadn't jumped, so I still couldn't imagine. Sally was shorter and thicker. We gathered awkwardly in the middle of the room. A double bed in the corner. A doorway to a second room closed off with a curtain. A shallow fireplace with a gas grate, and over the mantel a strip of Yale-blue banner lettered in white:

WHEN BETTER WOMEN ARE MADE, YALE MEN WILL MAKE THEM.

"The Whiffenpoofs gave us that," Gussie announced proudly. "They come down sometimes and we party." Gentlemen songsters off on a spree.

While I pretended to study the banner, H—— conferred with the King sisters. I heard the word "virgin" and the sisters' voices murmuring sympathy. H—— left them and drew me aside. "Twenty bucks," he reported. It didn't seem enough. Only twenty bucks to lose my virginity? Why had it taken me so long? "But I've got forty," I called across the negotiating space to the two women. "Nah, it's twenty bucks," one of them said, "we don't want to cheat you." We paid up, awkwardly. Then Sally and H—— were pushing through the curtain into the next room and Gussie was leading me to the bed. My heart was racing. The wind was tearing at the open door and the jumpmaster beckoned. The ground was a long way down.

"I'll just be a minute," Gussie told me. "You go ahead and get undressed." She studied me for a moment and her face softened. "It'll be all right," she said.

She disappeared into the bathroom. What was I wearing? Probably a white or blue oxford button-down shirt with the sleeves rolled halfway up, tan chinos, unbleached wool athletic socks and loafers—in those days the Yale uniform. I undressed down to my white Jockey undershorts and perched on the end of the bed.

Gussie appeared before me in a bathrobe. She let it slide from her shoulders. My eyes widened; her naked body was solid and healthy below her ravaged face. She bent, full breasts swinging, cupped my chin and kissed me, a smoky kiss that felt motherly. She noticed that I was still wearing my undershorts and smiled. "This is like taking candy from a baby," she said. Catching the band of my shorts at each side of my hips, she began skinning them down. I leaned back on my elbows and raised myself to help her. She had to work my shorts over my penis. I was already fully erect, pulsing. She knelt between my legs. Abruptly her hand was on me. She took me in her warm, wet mouth and I was weightless, not a thought in my head, joy diffusing through my body like water after thirst, and all my fear was gone.

Two or three strokes with her mouth, a quick warmup, and she climbed onto the bed and lay on her back. I followed her around and lay propped on an elbow beside her. She guided my hand to her breast. It was firm but fluid, weighted and warm. The muscles of her shoulders and arms had definition, I suppose from dancing. Her abdominal muscles strapped her belly, dividing around a deep navel. Her black pubic hair was curly and profuse. I could feel the stubble on her legs, unexpected but not unpleasant. In the strange country where I'd landed anything was possible. Gussie's body was a woman's body, generous and real.

"You need to make sure the girl comes first," she in-structed me earnestly—good advice. "Here, see," she went on, spreading her legs, moving both hands to her labia and opening them, "feel here, this little button, see, put your finger here and feel." I did, not knowing what I was feeling for, feeling wrinkled soft tissue like a hen's comb and lig-aments and a smoothness below them like the inside of my cheek. "You rub this, see," Gussie demonstrated, guiding my hand with her own, "until she comes. Then you won't leave her hung up." I rubbed a little bit, uncertainly. End of lesson. "Now you get on and put it in."

I got on, outlandish, lying on top of a naked stranger. Gussie scooped a finger of cold cream from a bedside jar and slicked herself and guided me in. I was used to my own cool hand. She was burning hot. I felt as if I'd plunged into an oven. A roaring began in my ears. She locked her legs over my back. I buried my face in her smoky hair, pumped, came.

With a cock of her hips she popped me out. Drugged, I slipped down beside her on my elbow again. "You should let a girl know when you're coming," she chided me mildly. "Then she can get off too." Abruptly her professionalism cracked and tears welled in her eyes. "It was your first time," she said, to herself more than to me. "And now you'll find a girl, get married, have babies . . ." As she had not and never would, I understood she meant. I was sorry for her and thought to comfort her. "I'll never forget you," I told her sincerely. She glared at me, sure I was mocking her, but I never have forgotten her and never will.

She carried her bathrobe into the bathroom and closed the door. I heard water running, the toilet flushed. My shyness had vanished; arms behind my head on the pillow, I let my detumescing genitals dangle. They were wet with her smell. I gloried in it. P——, a high school girl, was the closest I'd come before Gussie to sex with a woman. After weeks of necking, summer nights parked in her family car, P—— let me work one middle finger around her panties and inside. The first time it happened I'd carried that finger home like a trophy, flared my nostrils like the bull at the boys' home to sniff it, guarded it unwashed for two days. Now I had a profusion of Gussie's juices drying on my genitals, her musk mixed with the smell of cold cream in the air. I lay on the bed filled with happiness, one with the universe.

Gussie emerged from the bathroom brushing back her hair. She looked me over. "I put out a washrag," she said. "You'd better wash." I sat up. "You oughta use a rubber," she cautioned me. "To be safe. It's okay with me, but you never know."

I found the cloth and washed, reluctantly. A red rubber douche bag dripped from the inside of the bathroom door. I looked in the medicine-cabinet mirror and grinned.

We waited for H—— and Sally, Gussie on the love seat by the fire, I in a chair. We talked; I don't remember much of what we said. I remember noticing on the mantel a printed invitation to a headmaster's tea at Deerfield, past due. Some prankster must have arranged to have it sent. There was a snapshot of a burly sailor framed on the table beside my chair. "That's my sailor boy," Gussie told me proudly. "We just got back from a cruise."

Then Sally came out through the curtain and waved her sister over. They conferred. Sally went back into the other room and Gussie returned to the fire. She shook her head. "Your buddy's having problems," she said quietly. "Sally says he's got a little one. He can't get it up."

I didn't know what to say. I wasn't used to discussing sexual problems, especially with a woman. I switched to my student mode. "Does size make a difference?" I asked.

"Nah. Not to a woman. It does to some guys. I think that's what was wrong with Jack the Ripper. I think he had a little one and he took it out on the girls."

"Is my size all right?"

"Yeah. You got a good one." She winked at me. "The girls'll like that." I liked her saying so even though it contradicted what she'd said before.

H—— emerged looking miserable. Sally followed him.

"It happens," she consoled him. "No big deal. Better luck next time."

Out on the street I asked H—— what went wrong. "She started sucking me," he said. "All I could think about was where her mouth had been. It really put me off." He looked at me. "Didn't it bother you?"

"I thought it was wonderful," I announced, too happy to sympathize. The sun was shining. It was springtime. I jumped into the air and clicked my heels.

Two weeks later I went back on my own to see the King sisters again. Gussie answered the door. I gave her a box of chocolates, gift-wrapped. It amused her. She thought it was sweet. I'd fantasized having her again. She put me off. "I don't feel so good today," she said. "Sally's in the other room. She'll take care of you." I pushed through the curtain feeling rejected. Sally was sleeping on a single bed; I had to wake her. There was a double bed in the room as well and a man turned away on it snoring. I'd come a long way from rural Missouri.

Sally hooked us up and we fucked. The release I felt wasn't much more than I could do for myself. It certainly wasn't what I'd dreamed of. I'd dreamed of Gussie luxurious beneath me, of reliving the first time again. Not even Gussie could have done that for me. Maybe she knew.

I Experienced Orgasm . . .

I experienced orgasm for the first time when I was ten, climbing a rope in fourth-grade gym. I didn't know what was happening. I was light and strong, climbing a rope, pulling myself up and then locking my legs to reposition my hands, when I felt a sensation of intoxicating warmth spreading from my groin downward into my legs and upward through my trunk into my shoulders and arms, into my head, drawing down the muscles of my face. It made me feel sleepy and weak; my eyelids fluttered and I stopped climbing, drooped, barely hung on. I assigned the sensation to the same category as the shudder that sometimes shook my body involuntarily when I peed. I didn't immediately assign it value, good or bad. I didn't know what to make of it. I put it out of my mind.

After that it turned up irregularly when we were rope-climbing. I began to watch for it and wonder how I could make it happen deliberately and draw it out. I liked rope-climbing anyway. Now I looked forward to it eagerly: the smell of varnish in the gym, rushing to the side to uncleat the clothesline that hauled the big climbing rope up out of the way, releasing and lowering the twisted hemp thick as my wrist, lining up to climb, mounting the bulging knot that weighted the lower end. Sometimes the sensation came. Sometimes it didn't. When it did, usually three-quarters of the way to the top, twenty feet or more above the floor, I stopped and clung and drooped. It wasn't exactly pleasure. It was closer to a seizure, but it compelled.

I let down my relay team. We were an eager four against two other teams of four at two other ropes. I was anchorman—third in line—because I was strong and fast and could make up time. But my mysterious ecstasy seized me halfway through my turn and paralyzed me. I *wanted* to move, to keep on climbing; my muscles wouldn't obey. My teammates shouted at me to go on. They got mad at me. I was too weak to finish the climb. I slid down. Disqualified, we lost the race. I tried to explain what had happened. Fantastic tale. My teammates thought I was lying. They'd never heard of such a thing.

I wasn't the only one. I saw Dick Cavett interview Lily Tomlin once on television. He asked her delicately about a certain backyard clothesline pole she'd climbed in childhood. I suppose she'd mentioned it in one of her routines. She told him it ought to have a bronze plaque affixed in commemoration.

And how many more of you are out there?

When I arrived at the boys' home I was twelve and pre-pubescent. The housemother assigned me a bed on the aisle in the east wing of the second-floor dormitory. A bedside chest separated my bed from the next bed in the row.

One day not long after I arrived, a boy asked me if I "jacked off." I didn't know what he was talking about. He explained. That night, after lights out, under the covers, pretending to sleep, I followed his instructions. A few quick strokes, dry. When the sensation burst it burst abruptly, locally, painfully, like the passage of a Roman candle charge up its tube and out. It burned. It was nothing like the ecstasy of rope-climbing, which hadn't happened in years and which I'd almost forgotten. There was ejaculate. I don't remember how much, or what I did with it. But here was something new, a mystery, something to focus my curiosity on, something to learn.

Since we were boys and various—various backgrounds, various ages—coming of age preoccupied us. We watched for the least hint of pubic hair and offered it in public display. We showed off morning erections, ran contests to see whose erection could support the largest number of wet towels (the record was four). Yet the unwritten code that prevailed in that time and place stigmatized sex. Everyone masturbated but no one admitted it. Getting caught provoked months of merciless ridicule. Older boys, bullies, smacked you on the back of the head on the school bus, taunted you to tears. I only got caught once; I made sure I was never caught again.

I was a frightened child anyway—bookish, anxious, escapist, desperately lonely. Self-stimulation transported me to an inward place of altered consciousness that I could populate with sensation. Miraculously, my body could generate pleasure out of itself.

My record, an experiment I ran, was seven ejaculations in one day, the last time or two raw and sore. I was on house that week, which gave me opportunity, cleaning bath-

rooms and dust-mopping rooms and halls when everyone
else except the housemother—one housemother or another, they came and went—was outside working. I avoided
housemothers by hiding out in bathrooms and switching
floors. I wonder if they knew. Often enough my face was
flushed and my body trembling, stigmata of my crime, just
as the *Boy Scout Manual* warned.

I suppose some of them knew. I know Mrs. C——
knew. I thought she was beautiful. She wasn't more than
forty, tall, her skin colored between cream and olive, veins
prominent in her hands that shone in lamplight. Long, firm
legs. Arrogant pelvic crown that made her loose peasant
skirts ride high. I've thought it over. Sloping buttocks, the
shape and weight of them low. Something of a belly, a
splurge of fat over hard muscles. Big, pendulous breasts,
the only breasts that should be allowed at a boys' home; I
could imagine their dark nipples big at night as thumbs.
Yet fine, long feet and slender hands. A fine, long head
with a wide mouth, full lips and spiritual eyes, eyes wide
and brown and brimming, as if Mrs. C—— were always
on the verge of tears.

I could hardly bear to be in the same building with
her. She was safe only within her own room. It was a room
within a room, really, an apartment built along the hall
between the two wings of the dormitory. God, it must have
been a hotbox in those days before air-conditioning. It had
interior windows that opened into the dormitory wings.
The architect may have intended them for inspection ports.
That worked both ways—looking out, looking in—so they'd
been covered over with wallpaper, but the wallpaper fit
badly at the edges and admitted Mrs. C——'s light into
the dormitories.

We crowded those windows on hot summer nights,
trying to peek through the cracks, breathing through them.

RICHARD RHODES

We were beasts of the night forest watching in silence Snow White, eager if nothing more only to touch her long, cool feet. Mother and beloved, she was the one female in that hard, childish forest. I imagined her smells welling from the cracks with the yellow light, imagined her sweating curves that fitted my loneliness. How could she bathe, how could she breathe, how could she move to her bed and sleep with the gigantic din of our bodies and our urgent eyes thrown against the thin wood of her walls? Yet we never saw more than a shadow.

Lack of privacy at the boys' home made sex furtive. Without a room of my own, a private space to retreat to, I always worried about being caught. I found I could use images to focus my attention, to switch over from ordinary to erotic reality and stay there long enough for release. Alfred Kinsey discovered that sex criminals—convicted rapists, child molesters—disdain pornography. "What good's a picture?" they asked him. They started sex so precociously, he noted, that they never learned to masturbate. My heterosexual experience was painfully delayed; I learned to masturbate like a champion.

I masturbated to the plates of classical sculpture in the *Encyclopaedia Britannica*. There was a set at the boys' home, bound in fake leather, probably donated by some well-meaning member of the board of trustees. Years later, when I finally got to Paris and the Louvre, a lover rushing to meet a great love, I hurried to find the Winged Victory of Samothrace and stopped on the wide landing below her transfixed with remembered pleasure.

But for privacy I was crawling under porches, breathing dust dry as powder and beating back spiderwebs, or hiding out in haylofts, where I frequently came across other boys suspiciously nested and alone, and the *Encyclopaedia Britannica* was unwieldy. *National Geographic* sometimes served, when I could corner a copy. Although the United States in those days, the early 1950s, was as visually inhibited as contemporary Japan, almost every issue of the *Geographic* included paintings or photographs of bare-breasted native women. I learned to associate desire with tattoos, pendulous earlobes, Ubangi duck-lips and necks stretched with coils of wire. My tastes in fantasy, if not in fact, still run to the exotic.

Censorship never did work and never will. The glimpse of an ankle descending from an omnibus in a day when skirts covered everything but the tip of the foot aroused Leopold Bloom; in the years before *Playboy* and the sexual revolution I found high arousal among the corsets and brassieres of a Sears catalog.

Arousing myself with images was a learned skill. Identifying the right detail—a curve in highlight, a prominence of muscle that suggested the body's flesh and weight—incrementally increased arousal. Expression mattered more than physical detail. I always searched the model's eyes and face and posture for kindness, openness, warmth. I must already have assembled some inward standard of comparison, some subliminal archetype. Certainly any number of women had been kind to me along the way.

Words worked as well—worked better in those days, because they could be more explicit. (They seldom do any more. I've become more visual as I've aged, or perhaps approach erotic writing as I approach all writing now, having written so much myself, distracted by its engineering. I'm not often able to tune myself to verbal illusions.) After years of reading science fiction I discovered the lascivious historical novels of Frank Yerby when I was fourteen and put away childish things. In *The Foxes of Harrow* there's a scene where a black slave prepares her mistress to re-conquer her indifferent, philandering husband by bathing her, rubbing her with oil and stimulating her nipples with a feather. When I came to that scene I quivered like a reed in a storm. What stirred me wasn't the subtle sadomaso-chism of slave and mistress but the woman's awakening to arousal.

The little I could find out about sex I found out from books. Where sex is concerned we're all self-taught. An old, canny cruelty, an abusive authoritarianism, still con-demns us to general ignorance. Most of us never experience the intensity of pleasure and corresponding mutuality of embodiment that sex holds potential. There were no sex-education courses in school when I was an adolescent. There was very little information available in any case be-cause medicine and its funding agencies, not to mention government and the church, were and are hostile to sex research. Kinsey had published, scandalously, but I don't think his book was available at the library. I never came across it, and I'm sure I must have looked. Masters and Johnson hadn't yet been heard from.

Somehow I acquired a copy of Dutch physician T. H. van de Velde's *Ideal Marriage*, published in the United States in 1926, the most popular marriage manual in Amer-ica until *The Joy of Sex* came along. *Ideal Marriage* was wise and tender about love but euphemistically vague and sometimes criminally misinformed about sex. Van de Velde promulgated the sexist conviction that both partners in an act of intercourse should come to orgasm at the same time. "In normal and perfect coitus," I read in his book and believed for years afterward, "mutual orgasm must be al-most simultaneous; the usual procedure is that the man's ejaculation begins and sets the woman's acme of sensation in train at once." Impossible to measure how much pain that single ignorant sentence caused. It must have baffled hundreds of thousands of men and agonized hundreds of thousands, at least, of women. I took it for God's truth when I read it—wasn't it printed in a book? How did Van de Velde arrive at such a bizarre conclusion? From his own experience? From unsupported theory? Why didn't he check it out?

Discovering my body in the early years of adolescence was like exploring an astonishing and sometimes frightening new land. I remember catching a drop of the clear fluid that appeared at the opening of my urethra between a thumb and forefinger and drawing it out in a string, holding it up to the light, tasting its viscous salt. Other boys must have pursued the same examination; drawing one's thumb and forefinger slowly apart was a sight gag at the boys' home sure to bring a laugh, a visual metonym for masturbation. When I stimulated myself I often fantasized tasting and swallowing my semen. After I'd ejaculated, though, some obscure squeamishness intervened. In all those years and all those ejaculations I didn't act on my fantasy more than once or twice. It connects with a more frequent fantasy I used and still sometimes use for arousal of nursing a lactating woman while making love. Nursing while fucking is a fantasy common enough to support a small sideline of specialized pornography. In my case I assume the connection links sex to mothering, something from which my mother's early suicide—probably while I was still nursing—traumatically amputated me.

An incident with my violent, abusive stepmother when I was ten or eleven supplies a more sinister link. I was in the kitchen one morning trying to put together breakfast. There was a door at one end of the kitchen that connected to the small bedroom my father and stepmother shared. We didn't use the door because they'd pushed their bed flush against it on the other side. I must have rattled a pan; the door flung open into the kitchen and my stepmother appeared in a loose negligee, hung over and furious to be disturbed. She swung around to face me and began one of her rants. I hardly heard her. She was a small woman, but she had large, pendulous breasts. In her disarray that morning they hung exposed before me down to the nipples. Her cleavage filled my field of view and made my ears roar; I knew I shouldn't be looking, might be beaten for looking, but I couldn't tear my eyes away. She noticed I wasn't listening, dropped her head to follow my line of sight, saw where I was staring and smirked, paused in her rant, flounced, drew together the lace edges of her negligee and went back to ranting. Her new tone of voice made it clear that she was pleased.

I had confusing fantasies after that of nursing her, fantasies confused with sex, which I hadn't yet experienced and didn't quite understand. In my fantasies my nursing somehow placated her and disarmed her wrath.

My brother Stanley had found a set of eight-by-ten glossy photographs in that house. They showed one of my stepmother's relatives with a group of his army buddies taking turns being sucked by a big-breasted whore. The prostitute was naked; the men still wore their socks and shoes. Stanley showed me the photographs one day when our stepmother was out. "These are dirty pictures," he told me solemnly, tapping them for emphasis. I remember feeling shame but also fascination. What was going on, I asked Stanley—was the poor woman drinking their pee? He explained what little he knew.

That association in turn links my fantasy of tasting my semen to one of the casually cruel tortures my stepmother inflicted on me during the two years Stanley and I lived in her house: barring me from using the toilet from bedtime until morning in retaliation for what she imagined was my spying on her sex life with my father (I was certainly curious about everything, parental sex lives included; but my urgent reason for passing through her bedroom to the only bathroom in the house was to relieve my unreliable ten-year-old bladder). Lying awake for hours, clamping my sphincters until they cramped and pinching my penis to prevent myself from wetting the bed, I was unintentionally preparing myself for a lifetime of enthusiastic and prolonged self-stimulation.

So a drop of preejaculatory fluid can evoke like Proust's madeleine, calling up associations backward and forward across a life: confusion about body fluids milky and clear, their potential for sustenance, the sexualization of bladder control, near-incestuous overstimulation, a desperate dream grounded in torture of nursing myself with my own fluid substance. "The need to discharge rage through sexuality is a human burden," my psychoanalyst friend Leonard Shengold once wrote me. He thought my "precocious orgastic capacity" helped me survive my stepmother's psychic and physical assaults. I'm not convinced my capacity was precocious—preadolescent boys and girls both are capable of orgasm, knowledge that nursemaids have used in past times to put infants and toddlers to sleep—but I'm sure it helped.

But drinking one's own semen is also a fantasy of self-sufficiency, isn't it. Semen conflated with milk, the snake swallowing its own tail, self nurturing self; what boy hasn't dreamed at least once of sucking his own cock? I tried; to my everlasting disappointment, I couldn't bend that far.

There Are Styles . . .

There are styles of self-stimulation just as there are styles of intercourse. A group of us at the boys' home noticed one morning that a kid was lingering in a toilet stall. We concluded he was jerking off and set ourselves to catch him. The stall doors closed but didn't latch; all we had to do was tiptoe up together and push open his door. We found him rolling his penis between the palms of his hands like a coil of clay. After that we called him "Roller." He never failed to blush.

Usually men stimulate themselves with their dominant hand, dry, thumb and forefinger positioned nearest to the glans, making a ring that encounters the ring of the coronal ridge as they stroke. Somewhere along the way, probably early on, I switched to backhand. I see why; with my hand reversed, the tips of my fingers as I stroke successively cross my frenulum—the male equivalent of the clitoris—and stimulate it.

MAKING LOVE

Lying on my right side in the dust under the porch, in the hayloft or wherever I hid out, I used self-stimulation to generate trance states like those a later generation would harvest from marijuana; once I arrived in that sleepy, glowing dominion, free from the anxiety that usually nagged me, I wanted to stay there as long as I could. Stroking myself dry for thirty minutes or more was painful, especially since I had calluses on my hands in those days from farm work. I needed to reduce the friction.

To begin with I used saliva. It dried too fast, always just when I was making progress. I'd have to remember to let it collect in my mouth and then twist my arm around and spit into my hand; it was easy to lose in the transfer.

Butter served. It wasn't sufficiently viscous. Neither was lard, which we rendered at the boys' home from the fat of the hogs we butchered. I think I was smart enough to stay away from engine oil with its noxious additives. I tried Vicks Vaporub once in desperation. I'd already masturbated several times that day and the aromatics in Vicks ignited my arousal. Afterward, though, the residue I couldn't wipe away made my penis formicate. It felt like a swarming nest of ants hanging out in a cold breeze.

Eventually I discovered Vaseline, far and away the best lubricant for prolonged self-stimulation even though it's unnaturally viscous. I've stimulated myself for as long as two hours using Vaseline. Does anyone use it for anything else? It's immortalized in a limerick I heard in college:

A lascivious couple named Kelly
Stuck painfully belly to belly
Because in their haste
They used library paste
Instead of petroleum jelly.

And it figures in one verse of the Lulu song that I learned somewhere along the way through childhood:

> *Rich girls use Vaseline;*
> *Poor girls use lard;*
> *Lulu uses axle grease*
> *And gets it twice as hard.*

> *Bang, bang Lulu, bang her good and strong,*
> *Who's gonna bang my Lulu, when I am dead and gone?*

Tools might have intensified arousal. Even if I'd understood their uses, vibrators weren't available at the boys' home. A friend told me once that he learned to masturbate by accident, from rubbing against his top sheet while he was dreaming; he still got off that way at thirty. I wondered that he hadn't explored a more direct approach, but I underestimated him; it turned out that what excited him most was intercourse while retaining an enema his girlfriend had administered. It's easy to misjudge other people's tastes in sex. Sex is private; unless preferences are brutal, they don't show. Fucking in all its immense variety doesn't make you fat.

One tool I remember trying out was the metal hose of a tank-type vacuum cleaner. I conducted that experiment while I was vacuuming the office of the boys' home superintendent. I can't believe I dared—I was spraying, like a tomcat, marking territory. The man certainly would have shipped me off to a jail for juvenile delinquents if he'd known. The vacuum cleaner was efficient, I'll say that, and quick. I twisted off the wand, turned on the vacuum, took out my penis, wet it with spit, stroked it to erection and slipped it into the suctioning metal opening of the hose. The pipe swallowed me with a boisterous, pulsing slobber;

the vacuum motor began to race; my penis felt as if it were being pulled off but smacked against the inside wall of the pipe so intensely that I came before I even had time to steady down. The experience left me a little raw. I only repeated it once, in the relative safety of the dormitory when I was on house; all the noise made it risky.

What impressed me most about vacuum-cleaner sex was its efficiency. It got me off in no time flat and sucked up my seed tidily into its bag with the rest of the detritus humans shed. I like technological solutions to moral dilemmas. Eradication proved far more effective than centuries of prayer where smallpox is concerned; air bags and the abortion pill moot ignorant, tedious issues. The world would be a better place if men who felt horny lined up at rows of suitably decorated vacuum hoses to dump their loads instead of inflicting themselves on long-suffering women. I think, though, that I'd want the vacuum pressure reduced.

Inevitably some of us at the boys' home looked for sexual stimulation beyond the short circuit of our own hands. Precocious sexuality is supposed to be a sign of abuse, and I had certainly been abused before I was sent to the boys' home. But I'm not convinced that the furtive, frenzied sexuality of institutions is necessarily pathological. It looks more like a creative response to urgency and opportunity. "We was so poor," goes the old joke, "that for Christmas our momma cut the bottoms off our pockets so we'd have something to play with." At the boys' home, we lived not in a normal family with its consoling attachment and inhibiting incest taboos but among peers who were equally lonely and needy and who were genetic strangers.

Situational homosexuality in particular is common to all

single-sex institutions, from nunneries to prisons to armies to boarding schools, as anyone who's been confined in one knows. I certainly organized my share.

I wasn't attracted to my partners. We serviced a mutual need, mechanically. I had teenage crushes, but they were crushes on grown men I admired and wanted to emulate and hoped would love me. I fell for father-brother figures until I worked through that neurotic nostalgia (which is redundant, isn't it; neurosis *is* a pathological nostalgia) in psychotherapy in my thirties.

I'm trying to be honest, not defensive, and to distinguish one kind of homosexual relationship from another. I wasn't and am not sexually attracted to men or boys. If anything, I'm repelled. But other teenage boys and I masturbated and fellated each other in rebellion and lust and, probably, bare emotional consolation. At the same time I was powerfully drawn to creative, sensitive men who I daydreamed might substitute for the father who had abandoned me and the brother who had delivered me to safety and then (understandably) found his own friends and gone his own way. Often enough, I see now, those men were homosexual, but I made myself unaware of that fact, only wondering why at some point they backed away from the ingenuous gush of my admiration. Sexually illiterate, I didn't read their signals.

I don't remember how E—— and I got started trading favors. Given the risk, one of us probably said something over his shoulder like "You want to—?" and the other one barely nodded. We would have had to find somewhere to hide. The hayloft wasn't all that safe, and we were violating a crueler taboo than masturbation. The attic above the machine shed was a good hideout. So was the loft above the chicken house where feed was stored. Eventually E——

and I boldly claimed a space in the closet of the small bedroom next to the infirmary on the second floor of the school building. It was a walk-in closet, about three feet wide and six feet long, with a chest of drawers pushed against one wall that we moved forward and hid behind. The superintendent's office was downstairs, so using the second floor as a place of assignation was reckless. The closet was the one warm hideout we'd found. Our audacity secured us safety at least from discovery by other boys; I'm sure we resorted to the school building only when the superintendent was away.

In that nest that smelled of new carpeting, if not before in some bran-scented loft, E—— and I advanced from mutual masturbation to fellatio, probably on the reasonable grounds that we could do a hand job better ourselves. I usually volunteered to do E—— first, selfishly, so that I could enjoy the lassitude of orgasm without interruption when my turn came. I remember his small penis in my mouth like a straw mushroom, its odd, smooth rigidity, the faintly unpleasant smell of urine from his pubic hair. He usually sighed when he came and quietly moaned. He had difficulty with my larger penis; my ejaculation made him gag.

Once I suggested anal sex. E—— was reluctant. At the boys' home I'd learned to call it "cornholing," a garble corrupted from the rural practice when paper was scarce of using corncobs to wipe after defecation. We'd heard about it. The summer I'd arrived at the home I'd seen older boys in strange excitement chasing another recent arrival, an effeminate boy, in the gathering dark on the south lawn. Someone whispered to me that they were cornholing the boy. When the superintendent heard of the evening frolics he instantly shipped the effeminate boy off. In the baseball game of institutional sex it was apparently okay to pitch but not to catch. It wasn't an orgy I'd observed, as I'd thought; it was a gang rape.

I convinced E—— to experiment by volunteering to let him pitch first. In his anxiety he lost his erection trying. I took my turn. He was clamped as tight as I had been, and I've never found force arousing. Neither one of us made any headway. We gave up and went back to blowjobs, sharing the pictures we'd torn from magazines and folded into our wallets, crumpled glimpses of the indigenous peoples of Africa and Asia and ads for Maidenform bras.

One unforgettable winter afternoon when we were busy at each other's pleasure in our hideout behind the chest of drawers, we heard the front door of the school building open and the voice of the superintendent inviting someone in. A man's voice responded, not one we recognized. The two men went into the superintendent's office but didn't close the door. We were trapped. There was no way out except the stairs past the office. We pulled up our jeans, tucked in our shirts and froze in place, hoping our keepers would leave.

They didn't. They started up the stairs. I could hear my heart pounding. Down the hall they came and opened the bedroom door and walked in. E—— and I stared at each other wide-eyed and didn't dare breathe. I felt as if someone were holding my head underwater. The closet door wasn't even closed. We listened as the superintendent explained to the man, a candidate for housefather apparently, that this would be his room, that the couch opened out to a double bed, that he'd have a big closet, that there was a chest of drawers in the closet—

"Would you like to see the closet?"

God help us. The life I'd never get to live flashed before me.

"No, that's all right. I'm sure it's nice."

I knew then that guardian angels watched over me even as I committed terrible crimes.

They stood talking a little longer, an eternity. Then they left—the room, back downstairs, into the office; eventually they left the building. We waited a long time after that and then, still trembling, snapping at each other over precedence, departed singly and separately ourselves. We never used that room again.

Our close call was ironic. The new housefather, Mr. J——, a handsome, literate, well-spoken man, turned out to be homosexual. Later that winter a flu epidemic filled the infirmary next door to his room. I was among those convalescing there, drinking fluids and mooning over the love letters I received almost daily (I wrote more often than that) from a girl I'd met at church camp who lived sixty miles away. When all the infirmary beds were full, Mr. J—— volunteered to share his fold-out couch with one of the older boys, a sixteen-year-old who was something of a bully and who liked to show off his considerable genital heft. Uncharacteristically trusting, the superintendent agreed. It made us all jealous: Mr. J—— was nice, he had a record player and he smoked, which in those days was considered a manly virtue.

My temperature settled on normal. I left the infirmary and went about my days. Those of us who had recovered kept busy doing the farm chores for those who were still sick. One morning someone passed along the shocking news: Mr. J—— and the boy had run off together. It was the scandal of the year. Not long after it happened the superintendent called us together and lectured us. The boy was old enough to choose, he told us coldly; if he preferred going off with a pervert that was his lookout.

Eventually the boy returned, looking hangdog. The superintendent scheduled a meeting and invited the minister of the local Presbyterian church to speak. The boy expressed his remorse; the minister followed that public recantation with a rambling, euphemistic sermon about purity. Your body is a temple, he told us; polluting it offended God.

I was infuriated. At least the boy had found a little love, I remember thinking. At least Mr. J—— had held him and comforted him—I didn't dwell on the details. This Christian son of a bitch appears long enough to threaten us with damnation if we don't keep our bodies pure and then washes his hands of us and goes back to his cozy family life in town. Where he fucks his wife, I vividly remember thinking—I'd read Saint Paul—where he fucks his wife whenever he wants to, so who was keeping whose body pure?

I had turned to religion at the beginning of adolescence with innocent hope that Jesus, the ultimate father-brother, might somehow shelter me. I'm sure I first broke with Christianity after that homophobic, hypocritical sermon. I was outraged that men settled in marriage and family demanded of us, demanded of abandoned children, that we endure our desolation celibate and alone.

———————

One boy I played with boasted that he'd fucked a chicken. He wasn't risking much to tell me; given what we did together, he knew I'd keep my mouth shut. I'm still surprised he told me. I asked him how. He said his penis wasn't as big as an egg. It's longer, I said. He said he didn't stick it all the way in. I asked him how it felt. He said it was scary but it felt good. It didn't hurt the chicken. He said it clucked. It thought it was laying an egg.

I had trouble eating eggs for a while after that; it occurred to me that my playmate's semen might have been enrobed in shell and incorporated. Fucking a chicken sounds bizarre. Certainly it was perilous. I don't think he loved the chicken. It was a receptacle, wet and warm. *De gustibus non disputandum*. Out of curiosity I inserted my arm up to the elbow once in an old mare's vagina. The mare responded nonchalantly by raising its tail and dropping horse turds on my arm. I backed out fast enough.

Bestiality was much in the air around the farm. One of our mutts used to sneak away to the north pasture to hump pigs. If we called it off it slunk away with its ears down and its tail between its legs. We needled each other about the animals, particularly in the spring when the calves were looping their mothers' teats with their long, rough tongues and nursing—they'd suck anything, including each others' ears and your finger if you stuck it through the slats into the pen. But sex revealed itself on the farm in every season. It proclaimed its healthy necessity and universality, educated us to variety and made us randy. Whatever the delusions of religion, our senses gave evidence that we were animals like any other.

I watched the ram in ramming time mount five or six ewes in quick succession before it contented itself with sniffing labia to check which of its harem was next coming into heat. Maybe that observation led me to experiment with my own capacity the day I managed seven ejaculations. I watched cows mounting other cows in excitement at their estrus before the bull arrived in its massive authority to breed them. I watched the veterinarian estimate our dairy cows' dates of parturition by soaping his arm, working it up to the elbow in their rectums (scraping out a splashing pile of loose, pungent cowshit along the way) and feeling the size of their fetuses through the walls of their wombs. I watched calves born, ewes exhausted from birthing standing with dead lambs protruding from behind, rows of squirming pink pigs sucking lustily at a vast sow's production line of spigots, dogs tied like Dr. Dolittle's Pushmi-Pullyu, white maggots that squirmed on rotting meat pupating and swarming free as buzzing bluebottle flies. I saw the plumbed, tumbled, odorous interiors of bodies as well as the smooth exteriors and understood that we are not seamless and pure but interpenetrated and interpenetrable, that the lubricious openings through which we enter and receive the world and each other are worth our lives. However rustic my first omnivorous fumblings, I saw the difference between life and death and knew which one to choose.

Yet Through These Years . . .

Yet through these years when I was splashing every nook and cranny of the boys' home with sprays of musky ejaculate, when I was aggressively seducing boys, I froze with panic, like a deer caught in the headlights of an oncoming truck, when opportunities for intimacy with girls loomed up. I know at least one reason why. I'd learned, watching out for the minefields my stepmother laid, never to risk going over the top until I was secretly prepared and certain, and leading a girl toward intimacy was always an advance into the unknown.

I remember finding myself next to a blond and dimpled girl at a campfire at church camp when the leader called us forward to form the closing circle. I hardly knew the girl. It was delicious to cross my arms as we did and take her hand (and another girl's hand on the other side), but then she slid her foot inside mine so that her shin pressed against my calf. I was electrified. Paralysis set in. I couldn't decide if her move was intentional. (Why was I so stupid? What else could it have been?) Should I press back? Should I signal by squeezing her hand? What then?

My penis felt no such hesitation. To my horror, it sprang erect. I was standing before a bright campfire in khaki shorts, in plain view of the campers and counselors who formed the rest of the circle. I didn't dare look down to see if the bulge I felt was showing. I bent slightly to the left, the side my genitals dress, toward the girl, hoping to slacken the taut front of my shorts. That protective move brought the back of my leg into intimate contact with the girl's smooth thigh and my penis erected further, escaped from under the fatigued seam of my Jockey shorts and began creeping down my leg. Terrified that it might poke out its head and look around, I took emergency action. I shifted my foot away.

The girl stiffened beside me. Her grip changed. I'd rejected her. I blushed, blood rising like a detonation wave passing through. I wanted to explain that I'd been ready to fall in love with her, but it was too late. We chorused an amen. The girl jerked her hand free and turned on her heel and walked away.

I sat with dates in the back seats of cars with couples in the front seat necking and never made a move. I stood with another girl on the wooden steps outside her cabin at church camp for twenty minutes one evening, afraid to kiss her goodnight. She was someone I was serious about (but I was always serious about girls), a high school senior a year older than I. When the tension became unbearable—we both knew what was going on—I abruptly shook her hand. She burst into tears and ran inside.* At these and other

---

*"Thinking it was her fault," comments G——.

disasters of unspent youth I assumed I needed to ask permission. Many years later one of my partners, K——, who was considerably more experienced than I, explained to me with some amusement that people make eyes, send each other signals and usually don't ask. The Candide of the Midwestern boonies, even then I was flabbergasted at the news.

I made eyes with the girl with whom I corresponded so fanatically at the boys' home, but I don't think we went any farther. D—— and I met at church camp. She was tall and thin, and her gracile arms and legs covered with a light childish down took my breath away. Her lips were full, her eyes large and brown, her hair a mass of light-brown curls. I fall in love with women's voices and I fell in love with hers; she sang a solo at campfire in a high, hopeful soprano, "You'll Never Walk Alone." She dreamed of joining the Fred Waring Chorus someday. At least I'm sure we talked. I think we walked to campfires holding hands. I doubt if we ever kissed or held each other. On the strength of that delicate beginning, and because we lived too far apart to date, I wrote D—— nearly four hundred letters in 365 days. She wrote me nearly three hundred. In a romantic haze I thought about her for hours every day; I was sure she was the only girl I'd ever love.

Yet I kept her partitioned off scrupulously from my erotic life. I don't remember including her in my rambunctious sexual fantasies even once. I'm not sure why. I've never divided women into saints and sluts as some men (and women) do. But until very recently I split my life into before and after and lived more in the future than in the present or the past. Even as a child—especially as a child— I stripped past and present to a waiting room. D—— belonged to the future, out in the world beyond childhood, where life would be good.

There's a story that reverberates for me about Harry Houdini's having himself locked into jail cells. He usually picked the lock and escaped within thirty seconds. At the height of his career he challenged Moscow's dread Lubyanka. Thirty seconds passed, a minute, five minutes, ten, twenty. The great Houdini needed a humiliating thirty minutes to escape from his Lubyanka cell—because, as it turned out, the door wasn't locked.

My hesitation about making the first move with girls was like that. I assumed the girl was a lock I was supposed to pick, when she was probably as interested as I in opening up. Once, when another boy and I delivered our dates to their front porch after a Saturday night foursome, I devised a creative detour. He was the handsomest boy at the boys' home, but he turned out to be as inhibited as I at closing the sale on the evening. Maybe his timidity emboldened me. I drew him aside and whispered in his ear while our dates waited expectantly under the porch light. He agreed. We turned to the girls. "We've got a problem," I told them.

My date took the cue. "Maybe we can help," she said.

I blurted my brainstorm. "We'd like to kiss you goodnight, but we don't know how."

The girls looked at each other and grinned. "Oh," they said, almost in chorus, "we can *show* you." And they did, kissing each other instructively—they even closed their eyes—after which, ice broken, we paired off and necked sweetly on the porch until the boy and I had to go. It was a five-mile walk back to the boys' home and our 10:30 curfew was only an hour away.

I never used that line again. I should have. It embarrassed me, but it would have worked. Almost anything would have worked. A few years ago I asked my adult daughter how *she* dealt with the problem. "I just ask them if they want a back rub," she told me laconically. "But that's so obvious," I complained. "Yeah," she agreed after she'd thought about it, "I guess it is, but it always works."

———————

I still have trouble picking the lock, even with a willing partner. Once the door swings open I'm comfortable. I can think of at least six relationships across my life—six women whom I would like to have known in intimacy, whom I had reason to believe felt the same way, whose identities I would like to have commingled with my own—which my phobia almost certainly truncated. I grieve for those lost intimacies. They're experiences of human originality I'll never know, small deaths. "When the loss of someone dear to us . . . moves us," writes Claude Lévi-Strauss, "we suffer much the same sense of irreparable privation that we should experience were *Rosa centifolia* to become extinct and its scent to disappear forever." That's the loss I mean: of persons each a species, each unique, of gatherings of selves in my arms intoxicating me with essence.

That Was Childhood . . .

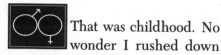That was childhood. No wonder I rushed down to the King sisters to have my can opened.

From here on, I have to deal with the question of privacy, just as therapists who write about their patients do. My solution, which I believe to be an honest solution, will partly denude the text. It will seem as if my partners were ghosts, barely present, and some of you who read these pages will notice that absence and accuse me of narcissism. I may or may not be narcissistic; here at least the problem is ethical. If I were writing about sharing meals with my partners I could mention their names and tell you something about them—age, place of birth, color of hair, color of eyes, education, parity, occupation, opinions, achievements, distinguishing marks, credit record, all the circumstantial evidence that passes socially for identity. But identity expressed in physical intimacy is radically divided from public identity in our culture. I can write about one or the other but not both together. I suppose I could invent false public identities for my partners. That would turn them into fictions, and since I'm writing verity here, not fiction, I don't propose to make anything up. "What we cannot speak about," as Wittgenstein liked to say, "we must pass over in silence." To write about what was private between us, I must pass over my partners' public identities in silence.

My partners, though, can't forget their public identities. Public and private are connected for them. They'll read their privacy here and probably feel that I've invaded it heinously. I hope they'll consider the paradox that by revealing *only* their privacy in these pages, I've preserved it. Only they and I will know who they are. And we know anyway.

The same sanitation of social detail is likely to convince some readers that I valued my partners only sexually. To the contrary, I valued my partners first and foremost as persons. Most of my relationships were long term; my two marriages each lasted longer than a decade; I cherish and haven't forgotten and could describe to you in detail much of the life my partners and I shared. But that's not what I'm talking about here. I'm talking about the part no one ever talks about.

To the best of my recollection, I've slept with a total of eleven women in my life counting Gussie and Sally King, five of them only once. Some people will think that's not enough to allow me to speak with authority; others will think it's too many to trust what I have to say. Here I am, and there it is.

That was hard to admit.

As it happens, for reasons I'll explain later, I've also observed hundreds of hours of sexual play and several thousand acts of intercourse between men and women, men and men, and women and women and have ghostwritten two books for qualified experts about enhancing sexual response.

———————

By the time Y—— and I became intimate I knew what female orgasm was, though I hadn't yet observed it. I understood that Y—— didn't experience it when we made love. She said it didn't matter. I didn't believe her. Orgasm mattered very much to me. It felt good. It relieved anxiety, which plagued me. It abolished, if only temporarily, the thick boundary that divided me from my partner. That I experienced it in our lovemaking and Y—— did not left the emotional account somehow unbalanced. I'd have felt intensely frustrated if I'd made love without climaxing. I was convinced the same must be true for Y——.

I did what I could think to do with my penis and my tongue and my hands (but I didn't think to ask, nor did Y—— volunteer). Sometimes Y—— seemed to enjoy what I was doing. Sometimes she stared at the ceiling and endured it. Sometimes she pushed me away. Gradually we made love less often, as I had feared we would. The boundary thickened further. My frustration and sense of isolation increased.

Summer came. Friends lent us a house. Summer heat kept us indoors. I thought then to ask. We were naked in bed, a fan blowing, the blinds closed. "Have you ever had orgasm?" "Yes." "How?" "I don't want to talk about it." "How?" "It's embarrassing." "How?" "By myself," Y——

said reluctantly, becoming upset, flushing, squirming, moving away. "When?" A wave of her hand: "Whenever."

I was stunned. It hadn't even occurred to me that Y—— masturbated. I don't know why not. I did, secretly, almost every day. Sometimes more than once. I didn't realize women did. I didn't know Y—— did. I'd never seen her do so and she'd never mentioned it before. Naively, I was elated. Y—— was interested in sex after all (as if she hadn't been all along). Afterward I understood what was significant about her admission: she'd finally trusted me enough to let me in.

"Show me," I said.

It took several days of coaxing. She was deeply ashamed. I'd found some other books by then, Albert Ellis in particular. I used their authority to convince her that anyone who had only one sexual outlet was probably neurotic.

Y—— stimulated herself lying on her stomach, her head turned to one side, her hands pushed under her body between her legs. She hardly moved or made a sound except for a sharp intake of breath, a quiet gasp, at the end. It was a pattern of masturbation she'd developed as an adolescent in her parents' house, secretive and consolatory. In the cool of a morning she let me watch. My watching inhibited her; she was a long time coming. But ultimately she did, and then she was crying with release and I was holding her, telling her it was beautiful to see and she was beautiful. I don't know if she believed me. I've never known a woman who wasn't beautiful when she was happy, but I've never known a woman in any mood who truly believed she was beautiful. At least Y—— had trusted me.

She opened up then and we talked, talked more than we'd ever talked before, talked like children, talked the summer away. Between talking we played. Sitting beside her on the bed as she lay on her stomach, I slipped my hand between Y——'s legs, covering her hand first to follow its patterning, replacing it later with my own. From Y——'s point of view I was working upside down. That was less a problem than it might have been. She found direct clitoral stimulation uncomfortable and stimulated herself through the covering of her labia instead, vibrating her fingertips from side to side. I could do that nearly as well by reaching through from behind. When my efforts brought her to climax for the first time we went giddy with joy.

We improvised then what I now recognize was behavioral modification. Before we could incorporate her pattern into intercourse she had to learn to allow herself to be stimulated lying on her back. She tried simply turning over, but the change felt too abrupt. We realized she could start by turning over when she was close to orgasm and then progressively earlier as her confidence in the change improved. When she climaxed for the first time lying on her back we celebrated.

Because I still believed Van de Velde, I still thought normality required us both to climax together during intercourse. I had a problem to solve before we could approach mutual simultaneous orgasm: I had to learn to delay ejaculation. I delayed easily enough when I was stimulating myself by decreasing stroking, reducing pressure, lightening contact with my frenulum and the ring of my coronal ridge. But intercourse was so much more exciting than masturbation that delay was correspondingly more difficult. Worse, Y——'s arousal stimulated my own, so the closer she came to orgasm the more difficult I found it to delay. More than once, to our mutual frustration, I climaxed just as she approached the edge herself. Then I had to stop moving in her long enough at least to allow the hypersensitivity I feel immediately after ejaculation to abate. And that was long enough for her escalation to orgasm, always an unstable progress, to collapse.

Masters and Johnson hadn't published yet; I didn't know about the squeeze technique. I didn't know that traction on the scrotum delays orgasm. I didn't know about pressing my tongue to the roof of my mouth. I could delay my orgasm by stopping moving, but that also frustrated Y——. I experimented with varying my stroking, which sometimes helped, although I responded so intensely to her arousal that timing changes didn't make much difference farther along the way. It helped not to look, to close my eyes, but I liked to look, liked the flush of arousal my partner's arousal added to my own.

We never really solved the problem. The right solution would have been to trash Van de Velde's ridiculous dogma, but I overvalued books too much to realize that. The most effective technique I discovered for delaying orgasm was mentally reciting the Gettysburg Address, which I'd memorized in high school. The recitation didn't always work. My brain would extract volumes of juice from Lincoln's seemingly dry and proper text, resourcefully squeezing out the hidden metaphors and sluicing me back to erotic reality again. The onanistic spill or paternal birth ecstasy of "Our fathers *brought forth upon this continent*" was particularly treacherous to navigate. Y—— became "this continent," her breasts mountains, her costal margins a Western rim, her belly Iowa farmland gently mounded, her thighs a valley draining into the wet underground hydraulics of her vulva. A half-remembered risqué song would start up in my head punctuated with a lewd whistle: "And on her [*whew! whew!*] was *West Virginia*, with those hills I love to roam . . . And down upon her *Wabash*, was my *old Kentucky home.* . . ." If I got that far, down upon her *Wabash*, I was lost.

Eventually we found a pattern that usually worked. I lay on top of Y—— supporting myself on my elbows and she inserted my penis (I had to ask almost every one of my partners to do that simple service, so much easier for a woman, who knows where her vaginal introitus is, than for a man; they'd never been asked before). Rather than thrusting then, I rocked my pelvis from side to side, my *mons* pressed against Y——'s, essentially duplicating the vibrating pressure her hand supplied in self-stimulation but with my penis inside and ready to launch. Straining, arching her back, gripping her thighs, extending her feet rigidly *en pointe* she drove herself through to orgasm, and if I had managed to hold back my own I let her key me (the opposite, I see, of Van de Velde's chauvinistic notion that ejaculation should trigger the *woman's* response), thrusting vigorously when she crested over into climax, racing a little desperately to catch up.

We did sometimes manage mutual simultaneous orgasm. It was wild, both of us moaning and thrashing together, deeply intermingled and lost to the world. But it was nearly accidental, booby-trapped with timing mistakes, rickety in the extreme. Far more often one or the other of us got passed over or left behind. I remember other times when I continued to vibrate my hips to Y——'s pattern while I ejaculated without thrusting and without pleasure because she was close to orgasm and I didn't want to interrupt. Which was fair—I came to orgasm much more easily than she—but frustrating.

I don't know when I understood that Van de Velde's ideal was ridiculous. Probably when I read *Human Sexual Response*. I should have known better. My own private experience should have taught me that single-mindedly pursuing orgasm, particularly a will-o'-the-wisp like mutual simultaneous orgasm, narrowed and limited pleasure. When I had privacy and time I always tried to make masturbation last, drifting in fantasy and building arousal along the way. It seems I'd helped Y—— bring her experience of self-stimulation into lovemaking but still secretively sequestered my own.

Nor had I yet learned really to let go. One of the legacies of abuse I carried with me from childhood was a deep split within myself. Part of me lived outside my body—outside of emotion and feeling—cynical and hard, believing nothing, trusting nothing and no one. Wherever I went, whatever I did, I observed myself simultaneously from a cold, pitiless distance. That split extended all the way down to orgasm. With rare exceptions I never quite lost myself in orgasm in those days; even there, when I ought to have been unconscious and unbounded, my cold observer intruded to watch and to judge.

Somewhere along the way—I don't even remember now with which partner—the split healed, at least in lovemaking. It felt as if a dense, muffling integument had been peeled away. Instead of a compacted sensation localized in my groin, my ears roared, my skin flushed, my eyes dimmed, my innards loosened and flowed, and I was one instead of two, I felt boluses of semen moving up through the root and shaft of my penis like Roman candle charges and then my entire body exploded and I wasn't two or even one, I was none and everything, I was there and everywhere at once.

But I can't for the life of me say how it happened, whether my ongoing psychotherapy accomplished some profound change in my mental health or I accidentally stumbled onto some trick of focus that had eluded me before.

I'm inclined to think the cause of the breakthrough was profound—it certainly increased my pleasure profoundly—but who knows? In the absence of reliable guidance we all learn sex haphazardly, catch as catch can. Maybe, fumbling as it were through incomprehensible pages, I'd managed the equivalent of accidentally teaching myself to read.

The Summer After . . .

The summer after I graduated from college, 1959, I joined the Air Force Reserve. In those days you were drafted into the peacetime army for two years unless you joined the reserves or the National Guard, in which case you only served six months on active duty. It was a scandal. People paid recruiting sergeants five hundred bucks for a reserve slot. What did I know? The father of one of my classmates, a reserve colonel, got me in free. The unit I joined was a MASH-style thousand-bed flyaway tent hospital stored in a warehouse on pallets, based in an office building in lower Manhattan, jammed with recent New York law school graduates. I was the only non-lawyer in my enlistment group. We flew to Lackland Air Force Base outside San Antonio, Texas, for basic training. We collected our duffle bags of ill-fitting clothing and gear and settled into ancient open-bay wooden barracks to be shaped into airmen.

I'd signed up to be a surgical assistant. That meant three months of specialty training at Lackland beyond the three months of basic. For the second three months I moved with my lawyer buddies to better quarters on another part of the base, closer to the hospital. Lackland was the main Air Force hospital. We rotated through its various departments, folding sheets and resharpening hypodermic needles in central supply, casting club feet in orthopedics, observing rows of hydrocephalic babies flown in for shunt surgery. Eventually we assisted in the operating rooms and nervously performed minor outpatient surgery ourselves.

By then weekend passes off the base were routine. Some of the troops bused into San Antonio on Saturday night, got drunk, bused back and spent Sunday sleeping it off. Some stayed on base. The one thing Lackland didn't lack was land. It was flat and dusty and boring, devoid of entertainment beyond pool and Ping-Pong and old movies at the base theaters. I usually stayed on base and read. I read all of Faulkner during my six months at Lackland even though I attended eight hours of school or training five days a week.

One of my lawyer buddies, A——, disappeared into San Antonio every weekend. I wondered where he went. He wouldn't tell me at first. When he got to know me better he filled me in. He went to massage parlors. It was sanitary, he said. If you ordered a "full-body" massage a woman massaged you and then lotioned up one hand and jerked you off. She wore a white uniform; it was all very professional. She caught your ejaculate in a towel.

I'd had other partners since the King sisters, but walking into a massage parlor was beyond me. I still had trouble buying *Playboy*. A—— didn't offer to guide me as my Greek-American classmate had done and I didn't ask to join him.

Then A—— found another sexual connection in San Antonio, one that matched an enduring fantasy of mine and inflamed me accordingly. He inherited two nurses from an old friend of his whose six months of training were up. The nurses liked threesomes.

By the time A—— told me about the nurses he was tired of them, tired of weekends in a hotel room having sex with two women at the same time. Incredible. I fantasized doing what A—— was doing and certainly never found it tedious. In my fantasy the sex was wonderful and the women were a delight. In truth, one of A——'s girlfriends was pregnant and had decided to have the baby, which was almost an outlaw decision in 1959. The other had recently been through an illegal abortion, whether because of A—— or his predecessor I never learned. Nor did the two women appreciate being visited exclusively for sex. They wanted a social life as well. They argued with A—— about how he treated them. He felt nagged.

While A—— was disconnecting from his ménage à trois I got to know another lawyer in the barracks, B——, who confessed miserably during a long evening of soul-searching that he was still a virgin at twenty-eight. Boldly I proposed to take B—— into San Antonio and get him laid. Get us both laid, maybe. I hadn't slept with anyone since I'd left New York four or five months before. I had A——'s nurses in mind to do the honors.

B—— and I bused into San Antonio and elbowed up to a bar in the nurses' neighborhood. A—— had given me their phone number, but B—— and I both needed a few drinks to manufacture the courage to call them. Finally I did. Two guys in town for the evening, I breezed, like to have a drink, and A—— had spoken highly of them and given us their number. It was the only time in my life I attempted such a crude pickup.

The nurse who answered was interested but suspicious. Where was A——? Why hadn't he called them? She hoped I didn't think they were something A—— could just pass along. No. Oh no. I didn't think that. We were just (crooning here, a little soft-shoe) *two guys in town for the evening, like to have a drink.* . . . The word "lawyer" didn't win her, so I tried "Yale." That worked. Her roommate wasn't home yet. She'd be around.

Half a hour after I called she came around. I seated her between us at the bar. We were three sheets to the wind but B—— was still seized with shyness. It was my turn to be the pimp. The nurse kept saying "Yale man." I was tempted, but I'd promised to help B——. When the nurse had worked her way through three or four highballs and caught up with us, she and I began to whisper conspiratorially. I told her what my classmate had told Gussie and Sally four years before—that a pitiful virgin had come to light who needed her help. A mercy fuck. After enough coaxing the woman agreed. I don't know why. A lonely Saturday night? I hope she was horny or at least amused.

She took us back to her apartment. I was falling-down drunk by then, cross-eyed, barely able to walk. She introduced me to her long-suffering roommate, who was six months pregnant and showing. I managed to imagine that the roommate might be interested in me wavering there in my Airman Basic blue wool uniform stupefied with Scotch. In any case there were only two beds in the apartment, twins side by side across a lamp table in the single bedroom. B—— and his deliverer crawled into one of the two beds; the pregnant nurse and I crawled into the other.

Through the murk of my drunkenness I heard bodies slapping in the next bed. Like a night wind blowing across a dying fire, the noise momentarily fanned my embers. The pregnant nurse had turned away from me on her side so that we lay in the narrow bed fitted together like spoons. I reached around her swollen belly thinking I might fondle her. She clamped her legs shut protectively and pushed my hand away. She was wearing a maternity girdle that shielded her groin. I fumbled once or twice at the girdle, heard bodies slapping a second or third time across the aisle, reflected smugly that I'd done my duty and passed out.

The morning after is a blur. Someone was up with diarrhea, a fetid smell drifting out into the bedroom. B—— stood awhile talking softly with his deliverer. I don't think my bedmate even bothered to speak to me. B—— and I stumbled out into the fresh air and caught a bus back to the base. B—— was quiet, happy, grateful, relieved. I was queasy with diesel fumes and the bus's motion. I never called the nurses again. I don't think B—— did either.

I know this is a terrible story. It educated me to the difference between fantasy and reality. It was the only time in my life I intentionally exploited someone sexually. Even remembering it makes my flesh crawl.

When I got back to New York after six months in Texas I was nearly broke. I needed a job. Before my Air Force stint I'd been a writer trainee at *Newsweek*. That was summer work. Back in New York in March, I applied for a permanent position. The alumni employment office at the Manhattan Yale Club turned up a slot for a writer at Radio Free Europe; I applied for that as well.

I had to find a place to stay. I approached a classmate's parents whom I'd met once or twice at Yale. My classmate was out of the country; I negotiated with his mother. She was a New Yorker, petite and sophisticated, a lovely woman. She agreed to put me up while I got settled.

I moved in with my military duffle and my college trunk. It was painful to sleep in my classmate's room, in my classmate's bed. A girl I'd loved had bedded him there when we were undergraduates to break off her relationship with me. I'd found out by snooping among her correspondence in a file box she'd left with me for safekeeping, found a letter she'd written to him. I called my classmate and ordered him to march over to my room. I was crazy. I hissed at him for half the night: "Did you *fuck* her? How did you like it? How did you like *fucking* her? Did you *lick* her *cunt?*" Awful. He did me the courtesy of hearing me out. Worse, I think we both enjoyed it. We'd read too much Hemingway. We both acted as if we were celebrating a rite of dark passage, two callow boys who'd stuck their fingers in the same pie elated at sharing a betrayal. Months later I overheard one of the dim-witted football players who lived in the suite next door telling his girlfriend on the phone that he'd heard me say nasty things one night about a girl, the worst things he'd ever heard anyone say. I stiffened and eavesdropped. Through the wheedling baby talk I gathered that the football player (speaking of nastiness) had called his girl to coax her into having an illegal abortion.

I don't remember seeing much of my classmate's father, Mr. E——. Either he worked night and day or he was out of town on business. Mrs. E—— invited me to join her for dinner one evening. We began with whiskey, as people did in those days. I was thin, five feet ten, 135 pounds, and I hadn't had much lunch. Two drinks and I was telling Mrs. E—— my orphan story, my story of lost love (I didn't tell her about her son's treachery), my hopes and dreams. She was enchanting to begin with; after the drinks it seemed to me she glowed. I fell in love with her. Then I had to ignore a swell of lust. She was after all my classmate's mother.

Over dinner, with wine, Mrs. E—— asked me about a play she'd seen performed at Yale, *Children of the Ladybug*. There was a copy in her son's room: had I read it? I knew of it. It was a verse tragedy written by a celebrated undergraduate, Robert Thom. She went on about it: how powerful it was, how much it had meant to her and to her son. Jealous of Thom's achievement—how many people publish Racinean tragedies before they're twenty-one?—I changed the subject as soon as I could. By then I'd realized that I wanted to write but hadn't begun to find the courage, much less the honesty, to do so.

Drinks after dinner. I had an interview at Radio Free Europe the next morning at ten. I stood to say goodnight. Read the play, Mrs. E—— encouraged me.

I found it on the bookshelf in my classmate's room and skimmed it sleepily. It was about a favored undergraduate who brings a classmate home for a holiday whom his mother seduces. When the boy learns that his mother has slept with his best friend he wades out to sea and drowns. The mother is left to contemplate the consequences of her hubris.

My heart raced. Was that why Mrs. E—— promoted my reading Thom's play? Was I the boy brought home to visit? Was she sending me a message coded in theater as people once sent messages coded in flowers? She'd gone to her bedroom, down the hall from mine; I'd heard her close the door. What if I acted out the story? What if I went in to her?

Which was all very well, but the truth was, I didn't dare. If I was right it might be wonderful. If I was wrong I'd be out on the street—jobless, unhoused and nearly broke. I turned out the reading light, seduced Mrs. E—— in fantasy and fell asleep. All over the world lonely people fall asleep alone on the other side of walls where other lonely people are falling asleep alone.

The next morning I woke and showered and dressed for my appointment. I came out of my classmate's room at nine. Mrs. E—— opened her bedroom door as I approached. She was wearing a silk dressing gown over a negligee edged with lace; I noticed her clavicles and the shape of her fine small shoulders through her gown. She said good morning softly, asked me if I'd slept well and then asked me if I'd read the play. I said I had. We made small talk about it. I felt the pressure of time; I had a crucial job interview to make. Was she welcoming me into her bedroom? Part of me understood that she was, part of me denied it. As my face reddened, as my tongue tied, I told myself that if Mrs. E—— wanted me all she had to do was take my hand.

The tension became unbearable. Did I say "I have an appointment"? I don't remember if I did or not. I remember what Mrs. E—— said. She said, gently, with disappointment but without patronizing, touching my arm, "You're a good boy. Go ahead to your interview." And sadly and reluctantly I left. "O love is the crooked thing," moans Yeats:

> *There is nobody wise enough*
> *To find out all that is in it,*
> *For he would be thinking of love*
> *Till the stars had run away and*
> *The shadows eaten the moon.*
> *Ah, penny, brown penny, brown penny,*
> *One cannot begin it too soon.*

Each of My Partners . . .

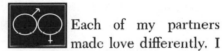Each of my partners made love differently. I made love differently with each of my partners. "Sexual excitement is a microdot," writes Robert Stoller. He means, he says, the doubly reduced specks of film which spies carry that conceal secret documents—"condensed masses of information, organized around particular themes." Words are microdots, music is microdots, facial expressions, symbols, love at first sight are microdots. (I fell in love at first sight with each of my wives.) How people make love is surely microdotted.

When O—— and I made love, the first of only three times through the one day and night of our brief affair, we licked each other's genitals; I lubricated her clitoris and stimulated it gently and directly with the index and middle fingers of my right hand; I lay above her and we thrust back and forth missionary style; but then she climbed aboard and rode me, this woman of delicate refinement, bracing herself with her elbows locked and her hands on my chest, grinding her clitoris against me hard enough to burn, cocking her hips back and forth while she bounced up and down, posting her pelvis as if she were riding a horse. As her excitement mounted she began chanting, "I want to come, I want to come," in time to her posting, "I want to come, I want to come, I want to come." Her face reddened and swelled and darkened with engorgement almost to mahogany. In its craggy darkness it seemed a man's face then instead of a woman's; it dismayed and repelled me. I had to look down from O——'s face to her body, drawing confirmation that she was female from the white curves of her belly and her hips, to maintain my erection. When she came, her pelvis fibrillating, her body arching back, her throat long, she didn't moan or cry out, but her chant resounded, coming true.

I said something afterward about her using my body to have orgasm. I meant the words only descriptively, but she was shocked; it hadn't occurred to her that a woman might use a man, only that a man might use a woman. She took what she wanted and I was glad that she had. She lived alone and didn't masturbate. That urgent riding, she told me later, was her first orgasm in six years.

———

W—— had an overbite which she'd worked into her scenario. She liked to click teeth. We never mentioned it. She offered it silently, I figured out what was going on and responded and after that it was simply something that we did. I didn't find it arousing, but I didn't mind it. It was better than the afternoon of necking visited upon me once by the girlfriend of a roommate. My roommate's girlfriend came over one day when he was away, apparently to check me out; her idea of French kissing, after we'd had some wine, was to flare her mouth to its full trumpet like a calla lily, so that our tongues flailed insecurely in a humid, winy bath of empty air.

There was a lot of drinking in those days. That's when my drinking started, building within a few years to a nightly sot. Only when I approached middle age did I learn to sequester it in fortnightly binges. Eventually, as I'll explain, I jettisoned it, one more life behind me. It certainly complicated relationships. W—— tried only once to keep up with me. She got crazy. I found her naked in the bathroom crouching beside the stool, paranoid the way I became paranoid the few times I tried marijuana.

W—— didn't have orgasm at first. I knew enough by then to ask. She was mortified. I had to promise I wouldn't be disgusted. Easy enough—why would I be? She inserted my penis inside her, clamped her legs around it, squeezed once, twice, three times and shuddered, as simple as that. Then she hid her face and wept. It horrified her; she believed it must be monstrous. I reassured her. How did she do it with her husband? She said she did it the same way except that he inserted his penis from behind. How was that possible? I wondered. She said her husband's penis was extremely long. Oh. I had to ask.

But W—— also volunteered to fellate me. I wasn't comfortable being fellated then; too many partners had provided it only as foreplay and then with obvious distaste. It was W——'s turn to reassure me, and she did, and nuzzled me through my dithering inhibition and brought me off, slipping up beside me afterward to point out proudly that she'd swallowed my come.

I never did know what R—— dreamed. I was too young then to understand that she wasn't orgasmic, at least not with me. She seemed to enjoy our lovemaking; she was histrionic and liked to be aroused. We made love every way we could think of, all the time. We made love in the right front seat of a snow-covered Volkswagen parked on a busy public street to prove that it was possible, laughing that the little car rocked, juiced by the risk that the snow might avalanche off abruptly to expose us. We made love during her periods, the smell of rusty flow metallic on our loins and my penis a bloody sword. We made love naked in the warm spring rain on the new grass beside a battery of Nike-Zeus missiles that shouldered toward heaven like a quiver of Cupid's darts. We made love in a cabin on the Maine seacoast, waves crashing on the rocks outside, gray light at the window, my penis between her breasts; her giggle reeled me in to consciousness after I ejaculated and I looked to find her squinting like Popeye, the orbit of one eye a loving cup filled with pearly semen.

The last time R—— and I made love, on an occasion of great importance to me, I reached around while we were coupled to touch her where we connected and along the smooth channel behind, pressed the small tight ring of her anus, wet my finger with her juices and stroked her there. She responded; she was genuinely aroused, perhaps for the first time with me. Did she let herself go because she knew it would also be the last?

K—— had brought home one-night stands from singles bars in the years before I met her, a way of keeping warm. She closed that door, she told me, when she collected two men one night who took turns fucking her and perhaps each other. Yet for all her experience K—— was preorgasmic. When we first went to bed I asked her if there was any special way she liked to be stimulated. The question startled her and she shook her head. Later she told me she thought I was asking her if she was kinky, if she needed leather or chains or shit or piss to get off.

We made love for months before she found her orgasm. It visited her in an antique bed-and-breakfast after a candlelit dinner, during intercourse, when I'd had enough to drink that despite the intense arousal she stirred in me I could have pumped away all night. I didn't know it happened; she told me afterward, uncertainly, having filtered the sensation ambiguously from the sting of our grinding. I hadn't realized that identifying orgasm could be so intricate. I think K—— found hers defensively, as a concession, to placate me.

When she couldn't calibrate it again in intercourse, or with my hand (she was shy of oral sex, ashamed to have her vulva seen close up and smelled, though in fact it was beautiful, dark and fleshy as a ripe plum), I proposed she try a vibrator. She did, alone, and after a few sessions it worked. She used a hand-held 110-volt vibrator mounted with a shallow cone of rubber. I tried learning to operate it but couldn't imitate her feedback-looped subtleties of pressure. Instead we improvised another way, after foreplay and intercourse that we both enjoyed: a finger or two of mine thrusting in her vagina while she cupped the vibrator's smooth rubber cone over her *mons* bellyward of her clitoris. I knew when she was coming, though she quietly sucked in her breath more often than she moaned: the vibrator's 60-cycle hum crescendoed in loud clacking when she forced the machine down to bone to peak herself and I could feel her pubococcygeus muscles pulse.

Later in our relationship K—— devised a further *frisson:* my index finger in her bowel, my thumb in her vagina pinching to stroke both sides of the thick interior wall—a three-point hitch if you count the vibrator buzzing above. When she came that way she bucked like a mustang.

I went through fads of position with K——, more so than with my other partners. I see why. She didn't require my penis to get off and she didn't do fellatio, equating semen with urine among her binary categories of dirty and clean. I liked her to ride me; she had strong thighs and pretty, dark-nippled breasts. She learned to read the signs that I was ready to ejaculate. She arched her back then to thrust out her breasts and reached behind me to squeeze my balls. It was like pulling the pin on a grenade; I yelled my moan and exploded.

At a later time and for some time thereafter we chose to enjoy orgasm kneeling. She went first, pressing her vibrator up from below; my thumb hooked in her bowel and my penis thrusting from behind substituted for the arrangement we'd perfected with my hand. When my turn came I held her hips and let the sight of her taut buttocks rouse me to pump myself unconscious, her strong hand reaching up to clutch my seeds triggering my ejaculation.

I learned about my partners from observation; even lovers seldom enlarge their microdots for other people to read. They usually don't even know they're carrying. Despite years of psychotherapy I've hardly begun to map my own fixations. Here at least is one small corner.

For as long as I can remember I've been compulsively attracted to women with Asian features. Living most of my life in the Middle West, I met very few; I've never dated or slept with an Asian or an Asian-American. The occasion

came up only once, with a visitor from out of town, but I
had vowed fidelity to a partner (or perhaps it was too close
to my fantasies for comfort) and reluctantly let it pass.

My second wife's features were slightly Mongolian.
That's probably why I fell in love with her at first sight,
across the room, before we'd even been introduced. Her
eyes had nearly epicanthic folds. Her paternal descent was
Slavic; her grandmother had come over from what is now
Yugoslavia in 1913. I kidded my wife that Genghis Khan
must have raided her grandmother's village. We visited
that village after we were married. It was full of young
women with features like my wife's, and I was right; the
Mongol hordes had swept through that part of Central Europe and sacked nearby Zagreb eight centuries ago.

Over the years, without pursuing its origins, I elabo-
rated my attraction to Asian features into a fantasy. Vague
at first, the fantasy grew less inhibited and more specific
as I aged. It became a story, a fiction. It will seem pedes-
trian; any number of men imagine they might find comfort
in the arms of Asian women, though I never craved a sub-
missive wife (my partners, particularly my long-term partners, have all been women of independent mind).

At its most florid my fantasy paralleled Paul Theroux's
novel St. Jack, or rather Peter Bogdanovich's movie version
of it: I own an Asian whorehouse and audition, train and
sample its girls. When I traveled in my work I played back
my fantasy at bedtime, masturbating to ease myself to sleep.
Often the girl I visualized myself auditioning was new,
recently down from the hills, and the more experienced
women of the house gathered around to assist us with skillful hands and mouths. Sometimes I even imagined taking
a new girl's virginity, though in fact I think the pursuit of
virginity is a vicious exploitation. The fantasy was specific:
it wasn't the girl's hymen I wanted, it was the exhilaration

of being the first to arouse her to orgasm, the very thought of which brought urgent congestion to my groin—her slender limbs stirring, a flush spreading across her neck and chest, her eyelids fluttering closed, her skin expressing a dew of sweat.

I trace my attraction to Asian features to my early imprinting on the indigenous peoples of *National Geographic*. Farther back is something dimmer but more significant, a children's book, *The Five Chinese Brothers*, that I read when I was small. I went through childhood without a mother and with a father away at work; my guardian and protector was my brother Stanley, not quite two years older than I. In *The Five Chinese Brothers*, five big brothers save a little Chinese boy in trouble. One of them can swallow the sea; one has an iron neck; one can stretch his legs; one can hold his breath indefinitely; one can't be burned (looking off in another direction through this small corner of my microdot I can see Shadrach, Meshach and Abednego silhouetted in the flames of Nebuchadnezzar's fiery furnace).

Several years ago I wrote a screenplay about Chang-Eng, the original Siamese twins, who were attached at the sternum by a strong fibrous band. (They could stand side by side, swim together, dance together—what a musical my screenplay would make!) Chang-Eng came to the United States as young men in 1829 from Siam, toured with Barnum, married sisters and settled down to become prosperous American farmers. Although I titled the screenplay *Closer Than Brothers*, it didn't occur to me until I began writing this chapter that the story of Chang-Eng links through the five Chinese brothers to Stanley and me. A pair of freaks who triumph over adversity. I suppose we are. "My work is like a diary," John Richardson quotes

Picasso telling biographers. From a children's book that I associated with my brother I got an affectionate, powerful screenplay.

I feel like Melville here, chasing down the whiteness of the whale. Why did I switch the gender of the Asians in my fantasies? One reason was to escape an incest taboo. I've noticed that I find women with pale, freckled skin sexually unappealing, even women who are otherwise attractive. My brother has pale, freckled skin; I assume that growing up with him instilled in me a taboo against his particular coloring that I subsequently overgeneralized.

Another reason, the more important reason, is that the change of gender allows me to sexualize the story. The bodies of Asian women are small by Western standards and relatively hairless, relatively childlike. Only recently have I permitted myself to realize that I embody innocent childhood in the figure of a young girl. A ghost child—she's Dante's Beatrice, actually—wanders the pages of my novel *Sons of Earth*, for example, giving comfort to the narrator, who's an astronaut trying to track down a man who's kidnapped his son. The young girl embodies not innocent childhood in general but *my* innocent childhood, the one I didn't have. I see that Stoller's image needs updating. The microdot is a hologram. Every area of a hologram records all the information available in that hologram redundantly. If you tear off a corner you can look into it and see the whole. Through this small corner I've been examining and beyond, indistinct in the distance, the central images loom.

My Asian whorehouse fantasy is a fantasy of release from the torture my stepmother inflicted on me when she denied me the use of the toilet from bedtime until morning. Here, I'll chart it:

I'm an adult and power- ful	:	the owner of the whore- house.
I take a young Asian girl	:	my child-persona
with the help of her	:	my brother, the five
older "sisters"		Chinese brothers, trans- formed to avoid an in- cest taboo.
Together we arouse her*	:	as I was overstimulated by my swollen, painful bladder
and give her orgasm	:	release: the relief of uri- nation I was denied.

Which isn't nearly all I could say about my Asian theme, but it's enough for now. "I doubt if the best poet has yet written any five-act play," says Emerson, "that can compare in thoroughness of invention with this unwritten play in fifty acts, composed by the dullest snorer on the floor of the watchhouse." As with the unwritten play of dreams, so with microdots—for this dull snorer too. Who knows what marvelous fifty-act plays my partners dreamed? And what about yours?

---

*Introducing a sadistic element: here I've identified myself with my stepmother.

After N—— and
I . . .

After N—— and I had been together long enough to imagine we owned each other, she had an affair. It began on a Christmas Eve at a lavish party some millionaire friends of ours gave. I couldn't find N—— in the crowd and went looking for her. I discovered her in a side room. The doorway into the room made a frame; at the center of the composition, glowing in the lamplight, N—— leaned across a low table conspiring with a dark man. I felt their eagerness to be intimate. Just as instantly I denied it. Later our hosts bused us to a movie theater for a private showing. I was drunk by then; so was N——. On the bus she introduced me to J——, who was an anthropologist, something like that. Someone who observes the native rites. I couldn't sit still for the movie. I left early, commending N—— to her friend, encouraging him to drive her home. Unconsciously pimping, thereby asserting a measure of control.

At home I waited up, getting drunker. I was young and ignorant and hadn't yet sorted out where I stopped and my partners began. I sat in the darkness chain-smoking, playing and replaying one of the arias from Menotti's *The Medium*, denying what I knew was happening somewhere in a room or the back seat of a car, singing along out of my range, begging with the singer to know where my lover had gone. When N—— and J—— finally turned up I stumbled to the door to welcome them. N—— was disconcerted. J—— played it cool. The woman went on to bed and the boys had a fine intellectual conversation.

That night N—— and J—— began an obsessive affair. J—— reminded N—— of her father, a dark, sadistic man who had abused her violently when she was a child. Father and lover even shared the same first name. N—— caromed back and forth between antipodes. Her father was a champion anti-Semite and J—— was Jewish. I was her good angel, my light coloring and Anglo-Saxon reserve like her cherished older brother's, dark J—— her bad angel. There are yet giants in the earth. Life is a dream and we squander our days contriving fabliaux.

N——'s obsession with J—— reanimated my obsession with N——. She denied the affair. I deluded myself into believing her denial until she turned over naked in bed one evening and I spotted a handprint welted on her rump. It seemed J—— had cuffed her when she'd refused him some surrender he'd proposed. And why had she? Isn't one point of such affairs plasticity, destructive testing, trying each other to see what gives? After I discovered that handprint and N—— admitted her affair I couldn't get enough of her. She was hot as a pistol; she glowed in the dark. We'd had trouble sexually since the first time we slept together. She'd be excited for a few days to no discernible pattern and then resistant and depressed for months. Now, envy fueling lust, I demanded that she dispense me at least as much time and passion as J—— got. I was sniffing after sloppy seconds, getting mine. Two men competing for her, two men performing for her, was okay with N——, though all the fucking sometimes left her sore.

We fought, of course. N—— reminded me of a mess I'd made the year before, a night of swinging with a neighbor couple that I'd engineered. You started it, N—— accused me, and she was right—I had. But I didn't carry it on, I weaseled; you asked me to stop and I did. I can't stop, N—— told me bluntly. Foolishly I took it personally instead of realizing that buttons had been pushed, it was out of my hands.

Then N—— woke up pregnant and it was time for adulthood again. N—— didn't like the Pill. Now it seemed J—— didn't like condoms. Problems with the poetry. They weren't natural. They reduced pleasure. But he couldn't pay for an abortion. He'd have to beg the money from his wealthy wife.

N—— went to see her Ob-Gyn. He confirmed that she was pregnant and projected the time of conception back to Christmas Eve. N—— and I discussed keeping the child. I almost convinced myself we should. N—— knew better. She knew we'd have a little J—— running around. Abortion wasn't legal yet. N—— went back to her Ob-Gyn. He told her he'd heard there were osteopaths and chiropractors in the city who did abortions. He promised her he'd help her afterward with any complications.

Poor N—— made the rounds. It was humiliating. She saw five or six osteopaths and chiropractors, all men. She had to pay them all and submit to their examinations. She was sure they were fondling her. Some coldly told her they didn't do abortions. One or two indignantly kicked her out. Finally she'd had enough. "Call your old girlfriend,"

N—— ordered, meaning the swinging neighbor. It was my turn to find a way to abort J——'s leavings.

I called T——. I knew she'd had abortions. I described the plight of an anonymous friend. T—— understood the code. She said Dr. X——, an osteopath, did abortions. "He's a sadist," she warned me, sounding paranoid. "He likes to hurt women." I discounted her warning. I thought she was exaggerating to get back at N——.

We found Dr. X—— in the phone book. He had an office downtown. N—— called and made an appointment. We scraped up five hundred dollars in cash and kept the appointment together.

Dr. X——'s office overlooked the busiest intersection in the city, on the second floor of an old building above a clothing store. Sad, heavily-made-up women with hard faces crowded the narrow waiting room. I realized they must be prostitutes. A frightened teenager and her indignant mother recoiled in a corner. I was the only man in the room.

We waited our turn. A nurse called N——'s first name and led us into Dr. X——'s office. He was settled behind a heavy desk stacked with papers—bald, middle-aged, with thick glasses. N—— told him she was pregnant. He didn't offer to examine her. He asked if the pregnancy had been confirmed. N—— told him it had. She wanted an abortion, she said nervously. Dr. X—— didn't bat an eye. He asked us who had referred us to him. I gave him T——'s name. He didn't indicate if he recognized it.

"It's two hundred and fifty dollars," he said.

"We can pay you more," I said stupidly. "We brought five hundred."

"It's two hundred and fifty dollars," Dr. X—— repeated levelly. He explained the procedure: two visits, twenty-four hours between. He slid a business card from a stack on his desk looped with a rubber band. "I'm going to write the fee on my card," he told us. "Then I'd like you both to sign it." We did. In that tactful way, for his protection, Dr. X—— recorded our complicity in a serious crime. He booked the appointments, we paid him and left.

We came back on the appointed morning. I'd called in sick and I remember worrying that someone from work might see me crossing the street. N—— was in Dr. X——'s office for twenty minutes. When she came out she was fine. He'd packed her uterus with sterile gauze and red rubber tubing. Tomorrow he'd remove them.

N—— spent the night writhing with cramps like the bad cramps at the beginning of her periods. I did what I could. There wasn't much to do. I got out the hot pad and rubbed her lower back. She wouldn't let me hold her.

I drove her downtown again the next morning. This time Dr. X—— sent her out through another exit into the hall. She called to me weakly from the waiting-room door. She was pale, the blood drained from her face, bent over in agony. I helped her down the stairs. "He did a D and C," she hissed at me between clenched teeth. "Without any anesthesia. I don't know if I can make it. He just did it and put me out in the hall. The son of a bitch. He pulled out the tubing. God it stank. This is just horrible."

I helped N—— across the street to the parking garage and into the car. "I can't stand this," she told me, collapsed on the seat, clawing at herself, writhing. "Get me some codeine. I feel like I'm going to pass out. Go somewhere and get me some codeine."

Those were trusting times. The republic wasn't yet at risk. You could buy codeine dissolved in elixir of terpin hydrate over the counter as a cough remedy, up to four ounces. You had to sign a book. There was a large discount drugstore on another corner of Dr. X——'s intersection. I jogged back to the pharmacy counter and rushed the pharmacist. "There's a woman in pain," I blurted. "She needs some ETH and codeine."

"I'm waiting on another customer," he told me fussily, annoyed at my boorishness. "You'll have to wait your turn."

I waited long enough to see that he wasn't planning to hurry. "She's in pain," I barked. "She's got terrible cramps."

The pharmacist studied me over his reading glasses. "ETH and codeine is for coughs. We don't recommend it for pain relief."

"Codeine will work," I argued. Arguing with this fool while N—— writhed tripped a wire. "*What are you?*" I yelled, loud enough to turn heads along the aisles. "*Some kind of goddamned sadist?*" And lowering my shaking voice again: "There's a woman in pain. She needs help. Help me."

The pharmacist rolled his eyes for the customer he was waiting on. "Excuse me just a moment," he said. I wondered if other graduates of Dr. X——'s reality school had staggered in before me. The pharmacist fetched my codeine, showed me where to sign the book, collected a dollar or two, insisted I wait for my receipt. I thanked him. He nodded ironically and I was out of there.

I found N—— slumped on the seat. I was afraid she'd passed out, but as soon as I opened the door she roused herself, snatched the little bottle and slugged it down. A pungent odor of oranges—the terpin hydrate—filled the car. I started the engine and drove off. I was shaking. Ten minutes up the road I sensed that N—— was relaxing. By the time we got home she was sleepy. I put her to bed and sat beside the bed watching over her.

Dr. X—— wasn't a sadist. He did his D and C's straight because it minimized complications. A few years later I noticed in the paper that he'd been arrested. They took away his license and sent him to jail for twenty years. They must have found his little bundle of business cards naming the daughters of the rich, the daughters of the poor. I wonder where they filed them away.

I thought I could save N——. She probably thought she could save me. The truth is, we were terrible for each other. In some ways, destructive ways, she was like my stepmother. If anyone had told me I'd grow up and go out and fall in love with my stepmother I'd have told them they were insane, but that's what I did. In some ways I was like her father. We thought we were the best that we deserved.

We both got out alive. I grew up a little. Not much, not then, not enough. You almost never know what you need to know until after you need to know it.

"As If
Inhabiting . . ."

"As if inhabiting the flesh," as Joyce Carol Oates writes of boxing, "were not always a primitive proposition." Come inhabit my flesh with me for a while. Is it so different from yours?

All my life I've used still and moving images of adults naked in sexual play for self-stimulation. Such images were illegal when I began using them. It was criminal to possess them. Today they're effectively decriminalized, but they're stigmatized politically. They're said to degrade women, though both men and women perform in them. Why is public sex degrading?

Nor do many people recognize masturbation as a legitimate form of sexual expression. For most it's still something to snigger at, just as it was at the boys' home where I grew up. Sex therapists recommend it to both men and women for sexual training but rarely endorse it as a practice beneficial in its own right. To psychiatrists, masturbation is a sign of immaturity, as if only sex that reinforces social bonds is good sex. Is it more immature to masturbate than to rape? Is it more immature to masturbate than to seduce? There's a lingering prejudice, a hangover from a crackpot theory that's been around since at least the eighteenth century, that jerking off too often is mentally unhealthy.

"How often is too often?"

"Twice a week. Twice a week is sick."

"How often do you do it?"

"Once a week."

I've never raped anyone. To the best of my recollection I've never even fantasized raping someone. I've never exhibited myself in the streets. I beat a woman once with a belt on the buttocks because she asked me to, but neither of us liked the look on my face and I stopped and never considered doing such a thing again. I like women a great deal more than I like men. How could I not like women when I perceive the inviolable child at the center of my being to be female? I respect women and treat them accordingly. Women friends and sexual partners have complimented me for doing so. G—— and I joke that I'm an honorary woman. I don't know about that. I know I'm a nurturing man. You're welcome to assemble this puzzle however the pieces seem to fit. The fit I've found is Montaigne's, that nothing human is alien to me, from asceticism and altruism down through primitive, urgent, polymorphous sexuality, all the way to impulses of murder and dismemberment.

We're all *bricoleurs*. We all make do with what we have, especially sexually. I had a two-year experience of late and tortured toilet training. From that childhood experience I learned that sensation stimulated but delayed builds to higher and higher levels of sensation until release can be almost unbearably intense. When I started masturbating, in adolescence, I began exploring how to apply my unsought knowledge of the intensification of pain to the intensification of pleasure. I explored at makeshift and haphazardly. No books guided me; I improvised as I went along. What I discovered or rediscovered I eventually brought to sex with partners as well as sex with myself.

I explored self-stimulation for most of thirty years, for half an hour or more almost every day—I was a self-employed writer working at home alone. "Your hobby," one of my wives called my private play. I suppose I might have gone to whores instead, or pursued multiple partners, but I've never found it easy to use people. I was interested in sexual arousal, not in catting around. For that my hand was a perfectly adequate organ. Such extended self-stimulation was obsessive, of course, a way to reduce the pervasive, free-floating anxiety of my post-traumatic stress disorder by focusing on immediate bodily sensation, a way as well to edit and revise my childhood experience of torture—sexual turgidity substituting for urinary urgency, ejaculation achieved prevailing over urination denied. The images I used to focus my attention were reductive and compliant. They were intended for sex. The men and women who performed in the films and videotapes I watched implicitly authorized their use in that regard. I wasn't expected to introduce myself, or make small talk, or smoke a quiet cigarette afterward. The erotic images functioned exactly as the photographs function in a food or a fashion magazine. I looked and took pleasure, vicariously.

Pornography has always been available to anyone with the nerve to track it down. When I was younger and it was only available under the counter, I was far too timid to seek it out. When I went off to college, *Playboy* became available, a gift at least of unambiguous nudity, though I had to work to imagine consorting with its airbrushed models with their closed, obviously unaroused genitalia.

I liked the nudes of art photography better and found them far more erotic. They were no more obviously aroused than the nudes of *Playboy,* but art photographers celebrated what the magazine scanted or airbrushed away: the texture of skin, the susurrant volume of curves, graceful hands and awkward feet, a belly's delicate down. They revealed rather than claimed possession. The nudes of art photography followed from the tradition of classical sculpture, with which I was already familiar, and made it possible to imagine making love to them, and I did.

I don't remember when, after the photographs that my brother showed me, I again saw sexually explicit images. During college, probably. They would have been still photographs, probably crude black-and-white photographs in a magazine of the sort you could buy in those days in Times Square. I'm sure I was overwhelmed, that my heart pounded, my ears roared and my face flushed. For some years I responded to explicit images with compulsive urgency, and so much more intensely than I usually responded to my partners that I feared I was gripped with a perversion. To a degree I was. But I was also responding to the difference between the genteel sex my partners and I braved and the raw sex of pornography. I didn't know how to merge the two. When I tried I was usually rebuffed. Only when I found a lover who was as eager as I to enjoy uninhibited, ecstatic arousal—much later in life—did I sort out the confusion.

Improving technology made the images more accessible. Full-color magazines succeeded black-and-white. I found a mail-order source of the eight-millimeter silent films pornographers call "loops" because they're run repeatedly in erotic arcades for men who drop a couple of quarters into the slot to jerk off in private booths watching them. I bought an eight-millimeter movie projector. Three or four loops, spliced together, assembled a thirty-minute film. I could stop the action at a particularly arousing image when I was ready to come.

Finally the VCR made full-length explicit features accessible at home (previously I'd gone to adult theaters to see them and then rushed home painfully congested to work from memory). I could fast-forward through the tedious, badly acted story bridges that pornographers seem to think they need to structure or pad their work. I could advance and rewind back and forth across the most arousing scenes. I could time my progress through a climactic scene so that my ejaculatory orgasm matched whatever taped scene aroused me most, the moaning on the tape and my own loud moaning merging convulsively into sync.

The attractiveness of the performers improved as well. The people in the Times Square magazines and some of the early loops I saw were flabby and pasty-white. Often enough the men performed still wearing their shoes and socks. How did they get their pants off without taking off their shoes? Were they performing ready to run if the cops broke down the door? Was the floor cold?

California's increasingly rigorous canons of tan and youthfulness and muscle tone challenged the pornography industry. I've seen hundreds of explicit films and videos over the years; it's rare now to encounter performers who aren't tanned all over and at least trim, if not in fact athletic—the women more so than the men.

Bisexual videos from southern California employ the most attractive performers of all. Such videos cater to male bisexuality more than female, but the high physical standards that gay men expect of their pornography influence

the selection of women performers as well. The camera
pays more attention than the camera of heterosexual videos
to the women's arousal. Settings are less tawdry—an elegant townhouse, a lush summer park—and production values higher. Watching such videos, I had to fast-forward
through long stretches of man-to-man oral and anal sex,
which I found curious but unarousing—more evidence of
the extraordinary variety of human sexual invention. Is
there any sexual possibility that hasn't already been tried,
any projection or crevice that hasn't been stroked or
plumbed?

The climactic scene in these bisexual epics is almost
always an orgy—a dozen attractive, tanned, healthy men
and women combining and recombining in increasing
frenzy until they all climax in what seems one great col-
lective ecstatic cry. A recurrent fantasy from my childhood
that emerged in my therapy and writing—an allegory of
the brutal overstimulation I experienced—imagines everyone on earth loving everyone else, no hatred anywhere,
everyone on earth fucking and sucking everyone else in
one endless looping daisy chain. And there on video was
a domesticated, softened, chastened version of that utopia,
images of real people acting it out before my eyes.

Not that tanned good looks automatically arouse. I saw
several hundred young, healthy male and female bodies
when I worked as a surgical assistant in the Air Force. Only
once, at the end of a long, exhausting day, when a corpsman
wheeled in a beautiful eighteen-year-old girl for an emergency appendectomy, did I have to deal with an involuntary
erection—an awkward problem when you're wearing surgical greens no heavier than pajamas. (I described that
experience to a circle of people at a cocktail party once.
One woman went white with shock. She identified with
the girl. She was horrified to think that I'd taken advantage

of the girl's vulnerability, as if I'd chosen to be aroused.) I wasn't normally aroused in surgery because patients were unconscious and inanimate. Similarly in an explicit sexual performance, at least for me, a performer's level of erotic arousal determined her appeal.

People who find pornography disgusting usually assume that the performances are faked. I suppose they'd rather believe that the performers aren't enjoying themselves. It's evident that the men's performances aren't faked, since they maintain erections and eventually ejaculate. Proving that the man isn't faking is what cum shots are for. Withdrawing and ejaculating over his partner's body is a low-tech special effect meant to authenticate the man's climax, which normally takes place inside, out of view. Sometimes the woman performer chants her encouragement—"Come all over me! Come all over me!"—as if she found being splashed with ejaculate arousing—and scoops up a taste of semen or smears it enthusiastically over her belly and her breasts. Sometimes she pretends the man's withdrawal has triggered her own orgasm, pumping her pelvis and moaning. I've noticed, though, that the women performers often smile spontaneously when the men ejaculate. It's a technician's smile—they're proud of their work. Or the smile looks maternal and approving—"Good boy."

But women performers often also show arousal. They lubricate, sometimes copiously; their nipples erect; their labia open and swell; a rosy flush warms their upper bodies. They register waves of pleasure with curious involuntary flickers of expression, as we all do, baring their teeth, jutting their jaws, curling their lips in ecstatic mammalian snarls. Their eyelids flutter and their eyeballs roll back. They mewl and whimper and moan. They begin kissing, licking and clutching their partners to automatic rhythms, clonicly. A few, more exotically, suck their thumbs.

Arousal isn't orgasm. I watched for a convincing female orgasm for years, through hundreds of hours of films and videos, before I found one. I've found only eight occasions, five of them within the past three years. The most famous is probably Marilyn Chambers's screaming, head-tossing, red-faced orgasm in *Behind the Green Door*. A dedicated team of four women prepare the way by stroking and licking Chambers's breasts and clitoris and labia. Then a muscular black man with a war-painted face and an African necklace of beads and lions' claws carries her over the top with a long, elegant, accelerating fuck. Through the orgasm the camera focuses not on her genitals but on her radiant face. It's wonderful.

Of the other female orgasms I've identified, most have also been induced by another woman or include women as helpers. Only one woman, of all those I've watched perform, unequivocally comes to orgasm in intercourse with a man without a woman's intervention—a slim, long-limbed, pretty young performer whose professional name is Nicole West. In a thirty-minute video in which she pretends to be an errant baby-sitter, she first stimulates herself to unfeigned orgasm with a vibrating dildo, then makes love with two men at the same time, fellating one while the other fucks her from above or behind. Then she mounts herself astride one man's lap and rides him posting, the other man stroking her oiled buttocks, until she climaxes, chanting "Oh yeah, oh yeah," in time to the peaks and sharply sucking in her breath. As soon as her orgasm subsides, the man stands, still inserted, and carries her around onto her back, bringing her face into view, and it's obvious that she's semiconscious and postcoital. Curiously, she hardly strokes her clitoris even when she's masturbating; she uses deep penetration with the dildo and then with her partner's penis to tug stimulation from her clitoral hood.

The video is unusual also in focusing more on the woman's arousal than on the men's. The men are more than usually sensitive to her arousal as well; one of them, for example, noticing that she jigged her left breast rhythmically with her hand to increase her arousal when she was stimulating herself, performs that service for her when she's fucking with the other man. By the end of the tape she's adrift, gone, erotically overwhelmed, flushed and loose and lovely to behold. She's one of the best examples I've seen outside my own bedroom of the sexual luxuriance that women are capable of. No wonder so many men deny and ignore that capacity; no wonder religion has schemed all these centuries to interdict it.

I'm disappointed, but I'm not surprised that female orgasm turns up so rarely in pornography. Not many of the men who work as performers seem to be sure even where the clitoris is, nor do they usually give it much more than a lick and a promise. A lot of them sound angry: "Suck my cock, bitch," they order their partners; "Take it, bitch, take it," they demand. Neither the cameramen nor the unseen directors seem to care where on the time line of arousal the women performers might be. The camera and the cuts come and go inattentively. The men ejaculate more or less on cue. Since I feel tenderness toward these women, and find their arousal arousing, I have to ignore the male hostility that mars many of the films and videos I watch. On the evidence of pornography, I understand why most of the women I know think most men are pigs.

On the other hand, I've never encountered any overt violence in any of the several hundred magazines, films and videos I've viewed. Once, a tape I ordered turned out to concern a dominatrix humiliating her female love slave by forcing her to have sex with a succession of men, but the acting was so bad and the punishment so obviously faked that the effect was more comic than disturbing. No doubt real sadomasochism is available somewhere on order, but none of the thousands of pages of catalogs I've reviewed offer it, nor have I ever seen pornography offered for sale that knowingly included performers under the age of eighteen. (In fact, commercial child pornography is so rare in the United States—not surprising given the severe criminal penalties it invokes—that the likeliest source of any mail offer is the U.S. Postal Service operating undercover.) Scientific studies that measure penile response to progressively more violent sexual scenarios confirm that most men aren't sexually aroused by violence any more than women are. The truth is, women (and men) aren't treated any worse (or any better) in commercial pornography than they are in commercial Hollywood films. It only seems so, because the sex is explicit.

The anger of many of the male performers of pornography probably reflects their marginal backgrounds. They may also need to generate anger to keep the juices flowing, to keep their peckers up. It can't be easy to fuck on camera, in awkward positions designed not for pleasure but to expose the connected genitals to the lens, with a crew of strangers looking over your shoulder and between your legs and telling you what to do. The entire project depends on the male performers' ability to sustain their erections, performance pressure that would shrivel most of us. The men in bisexual films are classier. There it's the women who more often seem tough and angry, especially when they're given a chance, as they usually are, to poke the boys with dildos: tit for tat.

Reading Joyce Carol Oates's *On Boxing*, I'm struck with the parallels. "The boxers will bring to the fight everything that is themselves," she writes, "and everything will be exposed—including secrets about themselves they cannot fully realize." So do sexual performers bring something else of everything to the klieg-lit bed. Fucking for money isn't middle-class work. "It's a very mechanical, physical job," Harry Reems told me when I interviewed him during the federal *Deep Throat* trial in Memphis, and it attracts mechanical, physical people—also like boxing. "Impoverished people prostitute themselves in ways available to them," Oates writes, "and boxing on its lowest levels offers an opportunity for men to make a living of a kind." So does pornography, for men and women both. That's the exploitation, if you want to call it exploitation; the performers may call it a break. Many of them are evidently stupid. Some are desperate—poor abused Linda Lovelace. Some—the best—are happy exhibitionists. Some, starstruck, dream of fame, not always realizing that what they will win is notoriety. "To enter the ring near-naked and to risk one's life . . ." writes Oates. To enter the bedroom naked and to expose one's sexuality . . . "They will know, as few of us can know of ourselves, what physical and psychic power they possess. . . ."*

The bourgeoisie has only recently begun to welcome pornography into its living rooms; the backlist still reflects

---

*Oates might not agree. At the end of *On Boxing* she positions herself among those who believe that pornography, unlike boxing, is a travesty and a fraud— "as fraudulent," she asserts, "as professional wrestling." She goes on: "It is not so much about itself as about the violation of a taboo. That the taboo is spiritual rather than physical, or sexual—that our most valuable human experience, love, is being desecrated, parodied, mocked—is surely at the core of our culture's fascination with pornography. In another culture, undefined by spiritual-emotional values, pornography could not exist, for who would pay to see it?" But cultures as spiritually diverse as Japan, India, classical Rome, Iron-Age Benin all produced sexually explicit images, often to celebrate the spirit in the flesh. And the sex in pornography may be crude, but it isn't fraudulent, nor is most pornography about love. It's about pricks and cunts. It's about lust and the body. It's about—it's a celebration of—being an animal and doing what animals do. At that primitive level, just as Oates asserts of boxing, it's "altogether real."

proletarian tastes. The unapologetically vulgar copy in catalogs of pornography, which I find hilarious, gives its proletarian origins away. It usually celebrates sex in trade metaphors; fucking is "laying hose," "laying pipe"; anal sex is "rear-entry" sex through the "back door"—the workman's entrance—"up the old dirt chute." Porn catalogers write like sports reporters. In a pool-hall video, claims one catalog, "Barbara gets a long shot in her throbbing love pocket." In a cop-theme video "Tori's giant tits sway as she rides Jerry's big nightstick to a hard-driving creamy conclusion." I'm not surprised that some women are repelled. They probably don't date construction workers and delivery men. Sylvester Stallone, billed as the Italian Stallion, grunted his way through a porn film once: you get the picture.

At the same time, I've learned from personal experience and from watching pornography that a gift or talent for sex has very little to do with other gifts or talents. It seems to be a separate intelligence. Any number of triggers—memories, words, gestures, sights, sounds, smells—can switch people over into erotic reality. How far they can go from there depends on how skillfully they can relax their inhibitions, focus their attention and read and respond to subtle physical cues.

Some porn performers develop incredible sexual skills. The late John Holmes sported an uncircumcised penis fourteen inches long at full erection and as thick as a Genoa salami. It's extraordinary to watch the full length and gauge of that penis disappear into a woman's body, sometimes a small woman at that—the vagina is an accommodating organ. "It feels like I'm having a baby," I overheard one of Holmes's partners telling him once breathlessly. Johnny Wadd's penis was a natural endowment (he seemed bereft of any other), but he'd also learned his trade. He counted several thousand partners to his credit. He could fuck one woman after another, of any size, shape, color or talent, tirelessly if not imaginatively, and come on cue. In one of his performances, back in the sixties (the room is draped in tie-dye, the sex takes place on a full-slosh water bed and everyone has hippie hair), Holmes brings one and possibly two of three partners in succession to unfeigned orgasm (with the help of the other two women, who stroke the copulating woman's clitoris and suck her nipples). He licked pussy like a dog lapping at a puddle. That sounds grotesque, but it was oddly charming, and effective as well.

Marilyn Chambers is equally skillful and far more attractive. Besides deep throat all the way down into the pubic hair, which almost everyone in porn learned to do after Linda Lovelace established its popularity, Chambers can easily take on three men at once—one vaginally, one anally, one orally—and bring them successively to ejaculation while attending her own arousal at the same time. Lying on her back, her head dropped over the edge of a massage table to align her mouth and esophagus, she can accommodate a standing, full-stroke oral fuck. In an orgy of the Olympians she once fucked John Holmes to exhaustion, taking him first orally, then vaginally, then anally, accommodating his heft adequately each way. By the time they were finished they were both flooded with sweat.

In real life, three-ways demand nearly impossible convergences of mood and tolerance and arousal. They're correspondingly rare. In pornography, which is despised in part because it reveals sex's raw Dionysian bounty and is therefore subversive of church, state, home and hearth, three-ways are commonplace. A raffish friend of mine once confessed to me in his wife's presence that he'd surprised her one night out in the guest house fucking a guest and accepted her invitation to join in. Before the night was over, husband and guest both found themselves occupying the same vagina. "He always tells that story," the wife complained; "it embarrasses me"—but she didn't ask him to stop. "I swear we all three came together," my friend happily concluded. Threesomes being threesomes, though, he tried drunkenly not long afterward to walk away from his troubles out to sea. I wasn't there that night to watch my friends fucking (though I sensed from their conversation that I might have had a turn), but I can watch two studs sharing porn star Amber Lynn's plump-labiaed vagina anytime, while blond, muscular Amber screams.

Why should I want to? Because a woman having orgasm is my microdot, the focus of my obsession with orgasmic release. Because I'm a writer, determined to extend the boundaries of what I know. Because I'm a primate, and correspondingly curious about the sexual organs and proclivities of others of my kind. Because I might learn a trick or two. Because it's forbidden. Because it turns me on. Why do you go to the zoo?

Pornography doesn't violate women or encourage rape, though it may subvert what pass in our vicious, unmerciful society for morals. It only demonstrates what normal men and women do together privately everywhere in the world, twenty-four hours a day. The crime pornography supposedly commits isn't the doing; it's the showing. "In our society," John Money told an interviewer once, "just as the Moslems have this incredible taboo on the visual image of the face, we have it on the visual image of the groin. It's undoubtedly not only hundreds, but thousands of years old, focused specifically on the visual image of the sex organs and their activity." Not even the sex organs generally; the law grudgingly tolerates images of the female pudendum.

The taboo applies specifically to the erect penis. I think I know why: people think it's the devil's tail, incontrovertible proof that we're animals. But we are, you know.

───────────

I'm alone at home. I collect videotapes from a cardboard box I keep in a closet. I have a range of choices in videos: images of blond women, brunette women, Asian women, black women, thin or thick women, athletic or fragile women, women with each other or with men or in mixed groups. I remember particular images and sequences on these videos in great detail and seem to have them mentally indexed, though I've made no deliberate effort to do so. Which video I'll pick is determined first of all by whether or not any is new. The half-life of an erotic image, by published experimental measurement, is about four hours, which is why people who use erotic images need to refresh their supply regularly, just as movie "addicts," news "junkies," "compulsive" shoppers, stamp collectors, cocaine or tobacco users do. But if all the tapes are more or less burned in, so to speak, then I seem to choose which I'll view according to drifting, lacustrine currents of desire. Perhaps I went to the movies last night and a particular actress— blond, brunette, Asian or black—caught my eye. Perhaps a clerk in a store, a dinner partner, a stranger passing on a street, a sentence in a book evoked some association. When erotic arousal encroaches on my mental world, as it does from time to time in response, I suppose, to unconscious psychological urgencies or obscure periodicities of hormone levels in my blood, the warm blush of rose on the creviced body of a ripe peach can summon an image from one of my videos of the rosy buttocks of a woman inverted in *soixante-neuf* with another woman on the deck of a California pool. Perhaps my partner and I made love late the previous afternoon and some subtle aspect of her response lingered in afterthought. Perhaps she lay loose after orgasm, her body turned and her face softened, one hand palm up and open, in a position that recalled Bernini's sculpture of St. Theresa ecstatic, St. Theresa visited by God, and that association in turn evoked the similarly softened face of one of the performers in the bisexual video *Heatwave*, the blonde on a yacht in the Caribbean who accommodates two men at the same time on a pool table and whose pale full breasts, warmed to translucence in the tropical heat, glow with a network of blue veins that evokes Bernini's marble. The world of erotic arousal is dreamlike; when I choose which videos I'll watch I'm already adrift.

I collect a bedsheet, a towel, a jar of Vaseline. The television is in the living room, against one wall. I spread the doubled bedsheet over the couch where I'll sit—I'll be working, I'll sweat. Punch on the VCR and the TV, set the TV on channel 3, insert a tape, collect the remote. There's a tremor in my hands, a lump in my throat; I can feel my heart beating.

My daughter asked me once if I'd ever heard of someone coming to lovemaking already fully erect—she had a new boyfriend. I told her yes, I usually did, and though we're candid with each other about sex she blushed scarlet.

So I usually do. I drop my pants and undershorts or remove them and sit comfortably on the couch. I pop the lid on the jar of Vaseline, lubricate my penis and begin.

I don't fantasize. Replacing that mental work, from which I'm easily distracted, is one of the advantages of using videos. Instead of building an imaginary world mentally, I watch the world the images record and slowly stroke myself. I can modify the video world with the remote—fastforwarding, rewinding, adjusting the sound. The video world is more limited than the real world, most of its information lost. To a much greater extent it's under my control, more manipulable, more predictable. I don't have to travel to get there. It's a highly specialized world, focused on eroticism, where people come and go specifically for sex. It includes no real people with whom I'd have to negotiate, whose feelings and needs I'd have to consider. It bathes me in no sensual smells, unfortunately—no lover's warm breath, no musky vaginal fragrance—but it also threatens no herpes or syphilis or AIDS. It isn't a loving world; it's raw and demanding and crude, and when I enter into it I'm raw and demanding and crude too, a side of my personality I prefer to release in private in this way rather than visit upon the world. Touch, intimacy and love I find elsewhere; if I didn't I'd be sick.

The real world around me falls away. I started to write that it's hard to say where I am, but as soon as I thought the words I realized where I am when I'm stimulating myself: I'm in my body, bodily. Where I always am, though I'm not always aware of it. Sex returns us to our bodies, whether together or alone. But sex alone, drunk on images, is different from sex with another person, as much so as another person's presence in bed is different from her presence in a dream. Personal boundaries—one's sense of where one is in space and time, of where *I* ends and the world begins—thin out and finally dissolve during sexual arousal. With a partner that means she and I interpenetrate and mingle identities. Alone, it doesn't work quite the same way. What seems to happen is that I stimulate my penis to build arousal in concert with the images I'm watching until I approach an orgasmic peak. That allows consciousness (and identity) to fade, whereupon through some mental invocation of virtual reality I enter into the images: I become the writhing couple, the ecstatic man and woman, the slick, swollen, feverish genitals themselves: their strokes are my strokes, their cries my cries, their pleasure my pleasure.

But I don't ejaculate then as the man does in the video. I back off, reduce or stop my stroking, allow the sensation partly to subside, reemerge sufficiently into consciousness to operate the remote and return to the beginning of the sequence or move on. And then I enter the cycle of arousal again.

How much time I spend at this process of hypnotic self-pleasuring depends on how much time I can spare from the rest of my life that day. If I have new videos at hand I'm compulsive about inspecting them, in which case I may spend ninety minutes or more. Through these periods, stroking myself up to the edge of ejaculation and dropping back down, I can feel my pelvic organs and my testicles increasingly engorge. I need less and less stroking to maintain a high level of arousal until finally even a light touch on my coronal ridge threatens to carry me over the edge and I have to avoid my frenulum altogether. Consciousness brightens and fades as I monitor the environment or focus on sensation. Sometimes, far along, I nod toward sleep, descending toward a deeper state of trance.

I don't only stroke my penis. Sometimes I stroke the lower margin of my belly, a circling caress with the flat palm of my other hand. Sometimes I lubricate the fingers of my left hand and reach below my testicles to press and stroke the buried base of my penis—the penile bulb— which feels like the pulses of a minor orgasm. Less often I squeeze one of my pectorals and stroke a nipple there. All these caresses add to arousal. They're limited because I need my spare hand to operate the remote.

When I'm out of time, or when I'm so aroused I'm in danger of losing control, I prepare to ejaculate. I choose the sequence in the video I'm watching that has fired my most intense arousal. That choice derives in turn from the lacustrine drifts of association that started me on this course in the first place. I'm sure I unconsciously consult the secret messages encoded in my microdot to make these crucial choices: I never match a man's orgasm, always a woman's (and if no woman coming to orgasm is available, a woman possessed of real or well-simulated frenzy, or at least a closeup of working genitals wet and engorged). I prepare to experience mutual simultaneous orgasm with (an electronic simulacrum of) a partner, just as Van de Velde advised.

I speed up my stroking and once again include my coronal ridge and frenulum. Pleasure begins to build and localize in my penis and groin. I start to shudder. The skin of my temples and cheeks crawls, the back of my neck. I'm still attending the video, aware of its pacing, matching it, as my eyelids flutter and my vision narrows and dims. Increasingly I'm *inside* my body, my consciousness compressed, my pelvic basin a collapsing shell, imploding.

At maximum compression there's an answer from the center, a response. It opens in a rush from the gathering that preceded it. My consciousness expands with it—as if a star collapsing at the end of thermonuclear burning had reached its point of greatest compression, when it occupied the least volume of space and time, and now was expanding outward again. It's explosive, a moving shock wave. It gathers from my testicles, moves pulsing through my *vas*, swells at the bulbous root of my penis and ejects in successive boluses up my urethra. When it starts it liquefies all volition and I begin to moan, freely voicing what I feel. My arms and legs jerk. My moaning increases to a loud animal bellow. The pleasure, my self, the swelling, the explosion burst out through my nose and mouth and eyes and ears, through my skin, from my belly and feet and back and buttocks and balls in wave after pulsing wave of heat and flush and I'm everywhere, ecstatically I fill the world. I come so powerfully that I convulse and momentarily lose consciousness; my ejaculate, released like the urine I was once forced to retain, sprays as much as six feet across the room.

What an Odd
Organ . . .

What an odd organ the penis is. A comedienne talking about men having midlife crises: when she sees a forty-year-old driving a Corvette, she says, she wants to call out, "Sorry about your penis!" That concentrates all sorts of complex issues—the penis and power, the penis and money, the penis and youth, erectile strength, erectile frequency, the gaudy elaboration of the stalk—but only because the penis serves as an icon for the whole package. What about the organ itself?

More than any other bodily extremity, the penis is a special-purpose organ, a thing apart. It's a fly-by-wire contraption, extended and retracted by thought alone. Boys discover that truth painfully in adolescence, when the merest nanosecond pulse of lust may actuate a mortifying public boner that no amount of wishing will detumesce. Learning to control his erections is as much a part of a boy's growing up as learning to control his bladder was a part of leaving infancy.

Perhaps for that reason, men tend to personify their penises. Robin Williams, the actor, in the movie *The Fisher King*, spoke of "letting the little guy loose" when he ran nude through Central Park. In its flaccid state a penis does resemble an embryonic body with a proto-head. (Uncircumcised men will immediately recognize from my embryo analogy that my penis is missing a foreskin, trimmed off without anesthesia in the delivery room for no good reason by a surgeon collecting a fee; an uncircumcised penis resembles less an embryo than the business end of an earthworm. "An elephant proboscis," Vladimir Nabokov elegantly analogizes.) Men say their penises have minds of their own, but men are geniuses at avoiding responsibility.

I've never personified my penis quite that way. I've occasionally made sport of its passing resemblance to a carp, its little rosebud mouth and butting blind head, by casting it for a partner as a kind of poor man's ventriloquist's dummy, working its opening by hand while I project an appropriately burbled, abject voice. Usually women laugh, but one partner whom I misjudged—we'd only known each other six months and she was young—was horrified. That time I'd taken the routine too far—I'd drawn little ballpoint-blue eyes on the bugger. My comic turn rebounded when we went on from comedy to lovemaking. I asked for fellatio and my partner agreed provided I washed off the little blue eyes, but when I ejaculated in her mouth she ran gagging for the bathroom; all she could think of, she told me afterward, was that grotesque talking fish.

I don't know how most men view their penises—it's not something they talk about. A gay friend told me he liked his very much and wondered why gay men were so often characterized as effeminate. *He* felt very masculine, he said. The truth is, most of the time the male organ's function is thoroughly utilitarian and so perceived, a length of tubing, a motorman's friend that confers on men the immense convenience, not vouchsafed to women, of being able to urinate standing up. The long lines at women's rest rooms attest to the advantage, although the design of public rest rooms reflects the usual male indifference to women's needs.

It's curious, in public johns, to notice from urinal to urinal all the different ways men handle themselves, more evidence that we learn our genital dealings *ad hoc.* The reeling out is more or less standard—unbuttoning or un-zipping followed by extraction with the dominant hand. The generations have divided lately between older men whose underwear has a built-in slot and younger men who wear unslotted bikini underwear and release their genitals by unbuckling their belts, unbuttoning their pants, opening their flys and stretching the waistbands of their bikinis down out of the way. Whatever their underwear, once men take out their penises (long or short in flaccidity, thick or thin depending on genetics and the temperature; I've no-ticed a few that were real hoses) they have to aim them. Some direct the braided yellow stream with one hand, some with two. A few bold souls piss at will, hands free, but even they take hold for the culminating pulses that are supposed to clear the line. It's never certainly clear, a citrine bead always lingers, but few if any men ever wipe with tissue as women routinely do. Wiping after urination is so rare among men that it isn't even factored into urinal design: there's no paper in the vicinity of those upright porcelain *pissoirs,* and their drains are suited for flushing only liquids. A child was beaten to death in New York in a recent year for wiping his penis with a tissue as his mother with the best of intentions had taught him to do; her boyfriend believed it wasn't manly, blamed the child and decided to beat the message home. Not wiping explains that little spot of wet on men's pants when they come back from using the gents'. I started wiping when I found myself going onstage one day in prominently spotted light khaki slacks to deliver a public lecture, but to do so I have to forgo the urinal and seek paper in one of the stool enclosures. Instead of wiping, men pulse, shake, flip or strip, some so elaborately it almost looks as if they're jerking off. Bobbie Burns had the last word on the subject, a verse a Scottish friend quoted to me that I repeat here from memory:

No matter how much
Ye shake yir peg,
The last wee drop
Runs down yir leg.

The penis is evidently a less evolved organ than its female counterpart. Unlike the vagina, which has dedicated orifices for micturition and for sex, the penis serves a dual purpose, the same tube passing both urine and semen. One step farther back along the brute evolutionary line removes us to the lizard and the bird, where both functions mingle with the fecal function that we higher primates take such infinite pains to distance. No wonder some women find the penis a little hard to swallow.

The psychological literature makes much of the male organ's vulnerability. In my personal experience the problem isn't so much vulnerability as sheer awkward helplessness. (The truly vulnerable parts are the testicles, "the two sea urchins," Nabokov calls them, although G——— thinks they particularly resemble kiwis, and feel, she says, like wads of Silly Putty in a goatskin purse.) The little guy's paraplegic. Along with its tender dependencies, the penis doesn't simply take its place in clothing like an arm or a leg; it has to be lifted and positioned, coddled, settled. It's like a foot going into a shoe—fussy and easily pinched. Men are constantly shifting everything around, trying to make the package comfortable. Watch your average baseball player. He's either adjusting his plug of chewing tobacco or adjusting his nuts.

Then there's the business of "dressing." Men wear their genitals to either the right or the left of the center seam of their pants, and the two sides have to be cut differently to allow for the bulge. "How do you dress, sir?" a good tailor asks, confounding the uninitiated. In repose, inside trousers and shorts, the penis usually points down—in boxer shorts that's its normal dangle—but some younger men who wear knit shorts or bikinis point their penises up toward their navels. I tried that arrangement once to see what it felt like. It felt unstable. My shorts rubbed against my frenulum and started up an erection.

Which brings us to the function for which the penis earned its diabolic reputation—not its cloacal function. Sex changes everything. One of the reasons men personify their penises, I suspect, is that they have to keep an eye on them. It may take thirty minutes to achieve a full erection or it may take only ten seconds, and the originating impulse isn't always conscious. Since public erections are considered shameful (at least in North America; I don't know about the rest of the world), men work to avoid them out of turn, much as women work to avoid audible public flatulence. There indeed is fragility, or perhaps contingency is a better word.

I'm lying on my back on a deck chair at a public pool, for example, G—— beside me taking the sun, both of us wearing bikinis, when a flashback pops up on the screen of my consciousness: of the moment in our lovemaking, yesterday afternoon, when G—— and I were reversed beside each other in *soixante-neuf* and she began responding to my licking by groaning with my erect penis in her mouth—groaning around it, deliciously mouthing it, a giddy contest we sometimes pursue to see who can distract the other's attention first. Now at the pool, tickled by this wonderful memory, I first feel a tingling along the line of my jaw, then a similar, answering tingle in my groin as my scrotum begins to tighten in arousal. My penis, which my sensorium had disconnected, so to speak—which had been invisible—begins to reappear. I sense it engorging. Fortunately it thickens before it lengthens; that progression allows me time to assert control. I realize that I need to abandon my unbidden line of thought, of G—— moaning around my penis, or I'll soon have to cover myself or leave the pool. I switch my thoughts away like an awkward conversation and silently ponder the weather. My penis disengorges, the valves in its venous return system that had partly closed, open and the hot blood drains away. A warmth lingers in my groin. I'm halfway along into erotic reality; to avoid a quick return to arousal I'll need to steer clear of erotic thoughts, triggers, switches, for some minutes to come.

If I'm not out in public, if I'm alone or with a willing partner, I can let arousal proceed. Then my penis continues to thicken and begins to lengthen, straightening itself out. The shaft engorges first, the glans later and only by degrees. A decade or so ago I noticed a constriction halfway up the shaft of my penis when it began to engorge, a constriction that gave it something of an hourglass shape. I was horrified. My first thought was that I'd finally jerked off once too often. My parts continued to function, however, and eventually I realized that the constriction was only a temporary phase along the way to engorgement. It went away with full arousal, though I still don't know—because I'd never noticed it before—if I've always had it or if I'd done some minor damage to myself.

Fully engorged, my penis is 5.5 inches long measured out from the belly, 6.5 inches long measured up from the balls, compared to a nicely nestled two inches or so when it's flaccid and cool. I've read that five to six inches is the national average. I have no idea how reliable that average is, since self-reporting isn't trustworthy, least of all in sexual matters, and the measurements would have had to be done with the penis erect—difficult to arrange in a doctor's office or a laboratory, except perhaps for the doctor. Madonna scoffed to a friend of mine that boys worry too much about the length of their penises, that women don't care. One of my partners told me that women care more about thickness than length "since that's what they feel." My guess is that women respond to all sorts of variables, depending on what they've conditioned themselves to find arousing, much as men respond to variation in breasts. Erect penises sport veins and varicosities and there's a great variety in shape and coloring as well. My glans happens to be shaped like a Second World War Italian soldier's helmet, but I've seen glanses that were flattened, spade-shaped, domed symmetrically like bells or elongated up narrowly like olives. I lean about ten degrees to the left, another common variable I've never heard discussed (I knew a guy in the Air Force who sported a full 45-degree bend). The penis isn't a "love muscle," of course, as Mario Puzo calls it in *The Godfather;* it's an automated sponge, though that's difficult to believe when it's fully erect, hard as a piece of gristle and as unbending.

At full arousal, swollen and pulsing, veins standing out on the shaft like strangler figs, the glans purplish, thickened and bulged to twice its normal size, sending back powerful sensations, the penis is a thing to behold. Then it seems least of all an extension of the body. It seems some kind of power unit strapped on, no longer contiguous with the rest of the body's smooth container but abrupt and functional and separate, a bizarre pseudopod extended from the glandular interior, a pump pulsing with hydraulics, a remote submersible prepared to descend into the depths, a docked moon lander.

What an odd organ. Having a penis is like owning a cat.

One Summer
Morning . . .

One summer morning in 1981 I found a catalog in my mail describing traveling weekend workshops for health-science professionals. I opened it idly and paged through. A headline caught my eye:

EXPANDING SEXUAL POTENTIALITIES FOR OPTIMUM
HEALTH

The workshop was subtitled "New Methods and Procedures for Achieving and Extending Sexual Orgasm." I'd never heard of extending orgasm. I read on.

The text that followed argued that we live in a society where reducing pain is acceptable but deliberately seeking pleasure is not. It said that sex therapy so far has emphasized fixing problems rather than increasing potential. It cited new evidence that "males and females are capable of

orgasmic functioning vastly beyond what has been tradi-
tionally known or reported by Masters and Johnson."

Two columns of curriculum summary came next. Nothing out of the ordinary for such seminars until Sunday
afternoon, the second day of the workshop, when this:

> Clinical video feature: Demonstration of 30 minutes of con-
> tinuous female orgasm by a sex-researcher physician on his
> wife.

That knocked me down. Seymour Fisher's 1973 study *The
Female Orgasm*, which was based on interviews with several hundred women, reported an average duration of female orgasm of six to ten seconds, with "a few extreme
cases" extending "more than 20 seconds." Before Fisher,
Masters and Johnson had reported a similar average, but
discovered a few women among their research subjects
whose orgasms sometimes lasted for up to a minute. Masters and Johnson isolated that unusual culmination with a
Latin name, as if it were a new species: *status orgasmus*.
Now someone named Alan P. Brauer, M.D., University of
Michigan, clinical assistant professor at Stanford Medical
School, founder of the biofeedback and stress reduction
center there, and his wife Donna Brauer, a trained psy-
chotherapist, purported to offer videotaped proof that a
woman's orgasm could continue for as long as thirty minutes.

I decided to sign up for the workshop. I sometimes
wrote for *Playboy*. I called an editor there and proposed
to do a story. He agreed, which paid my way.

I flew to Chicago on a Friday afternoon and checked
into a lakeshore hotel. I bumped into the Brauers on the
elevator that evening and looked them over (I recognized
Alan Brauer from his photograph in the catalog). Brauer

was pale, not tall; he had a full head of curly black hair, a full mustache, a slight overbite and an antic look in his eye. He reminded me a little of Tenniel's Mad Hatter in *Alice in Wonderland*. His wife was a tall, willowy champagne blonde—a native Californian, as it turned out.

Over the next two days I sat with about forty other people, most of them therapists and counselors, listening to the Brauers and watching videos. Casual documentary catalogs of genitalia desensitized us to explicit images and reminded us of how various human genitals can be, as different one from another as faces. Wardell Pomeroy, Alfred Kinsey's associate, showed us how to take a sex history the Kinsey way. (Kinsey and Pomeroy once drove from Indiana all the way to the desert Southwest to collect a particularly ornate sexual history they'd heard about— we'd call it a history of extreme sexual abuse today. "It astounded even us, who had heard everything," Pomeroy recalls in a memoir. The man they interviewed was a college graduate with a responsible government job, sixty-three years old. He'd kept careful records; the interview lasted seventeen hours. His grandmother had taken his hetero-sexual virginity, his father his homosexual virginity. He'd had sex with seventeen of thirty-three family members. His sexual relations extended to some two hundred preadoles-cent females, six hundred preadolescent males and many species of animals. He told the two men he could mastur-bate from flaccidity to ejaculation in ten seconds. They didn't believe him. "Whereupon our subject calmly dem-onstrated it to us." Who knows what our neighbors do?) For advanced anatomy we learned that female orgasm in-volves contractions not only of the muscles of the outer third of the vagina and of the anus but also of the uterus, and that male orgasm, though most men perceive it to be continuous, is not a single but a two-stage process, a plateau stage of intense sensation culminating in a sense of ejaculatory inevitability, and ejaculation itself. We watched a series of German videos demonstrating the several signs of female sexual response. We watched a video of men discussing and demonstrating masturbation.

Sunday afternoon came around. "We prefer to look at sex as something that can get better and better," Brauer began the main event. "It's very seldom looked at this way. It was bad enough, a lot of people thought, to look at *dysfunction,* much less how to make sex better. But it can be made better, much better." He cited the official duration of female orgasm, concluding with the brave sixty seconds of *status orgasmus.*

Donna Brauer smiled. "Would you believe four hours?"

Brauer wheeled out a portable blackboard and diagramed a single peak of orgasm. Then he diagramed a sine wave of multiple orgasms. Finally he diagramed a steep line of arousal that crossed the threshold of orgasm and continued to rise along a more gradual slope. "We've seen a longer response based on uterine contractions. These turn up in women in trusting states with a partner. We find that women can continue to higher and higher states of arousal, with continuous contractions that are obvious and externally visible and that can be felt through the lower abdominal wall. These are involuntary reflexes, and the woman always reports she's not doing anything, simply *allowing* something to happen."

It was time for the clinical video feature. Curtains drawn and lights out. Now we would see.

A gynecological examining table draped with a white sheet. A row of observers—students—in folding chairs to one side. A deep voice off-camera, directing.

A slim man in a tank top and jeans leads a young woman into the room. She's pretty—tanned and naked. The man is a doctor. The off-camera voice introduces him: Marc. The woman is his wife: Susan. Marc helps Susan onto the table. She sits looking toward the camera languidly while he points out the normal pink of her eyelids, a reference point he asks us to note for the changes we'll see.

Susan lies down on her back. Marc plays lightly with one of her nipples and she begins . . . pulsing. Slight involuntary movements of her arms, her hands, her belly, her legs. It's obvious that she's highly aroused. Her husband grazes the hair on her *mons* with his fingertips. "Hair is an extension of the epidermis," he says, "and the epidermis is a sense organ." Susan's pulsing increases.

Marc sits down beside his wife on a stool, facing the camera. Susan sets her feet into the stirrups of the examining table and her thighs open before us. Her husband lubricates the thumb and index finger of his right hand with Vaseline. He spreads Susan's labia, takes time to identify the structures of her genital anatomy and starts gently, slowly, stroking her clitoris. She pulses more intensely and begins to moan.

The off-camera voice asks if anyone doubts that Susan is in extended orgasm. A young woman says, "I can see she's turned on, but I don't know."

Marc invites the young woman up to see. "Touch her thigh," he says. The woman hesitates. "Go ahead. It's okay." The woman does, feels the shudders there and returns to her chair convinced, shaking her head.

Marc takes Susan up to highs where she moans and involuntarily moves to flex her entire body. He restrains her gently with the arm of his caressing hand. With the index finger of his other hand he sweeps the inner wall of his wife's vagina. Her hands flutter into the air and her feet curl downward in reflex.

Moved by the beauty of another human being's pleasure, I discovered that there were tears in my eyes.

Finally Susan sits up. Marc points out her eyelids.
They're colored so intensely they look bruised. "They're
engorged," Marc says. "That's what eyeshadow is about."
Susan looks peaceful. She's dosed with endorphins and still
pulsing. The two kiss and walk away together, holding
hands.

The lights came on. We were silent, stunned. I saw
grins. I saw anger. Not many questions. One comment from
a gynecologist helped me understand the anger. "If you
give the woman this," the gynecologist called out in a Span-
ish accent, angrily, "she will be wanting it all the time, and
you know no man can handle that." We'd watched a man
handling it, but the doctor didn't believe his eyes.

The problem with sex, Donna Brauer countered, even
among couples trained in extending orgasm, wasn't wanting
it all the time, it was budgeting enough time from busy
lives to have it once in a while.

The Brauers hurried on to discuss extending male orgasm. They had no video to show; they hadn't produced
one yet.

"If you conceive of every man, regardless of his sexual
endurance, as being essentially an early ejaculator," Brauer
said, "you can see how we proceed in our training. The
man participates passively, much as the woman does; you
have two attentions on one nervous system, just as we saw
with Susan in the film. A man can't be quite as passive as
a woman, because he has to monitor where he is in order
to avoid going over the edge and ejaculating. What happens
is this: the woman, using a combination of manual and oral
stimulation, takes the man up to a point near ejaculation—
to the emission stage, where he's secreting clear fluid—

and then stops stimulating or uses scrotal traction to allow his level of arousal to drop slightly. Then she takes him up again. She does that three to nine times in a given hour-long session over a period of one to three months. Within that time period, a man can learn better control, how to stay in the highly pleasurable plateau stage next to ejaculation. Once he learns that control, he'll find his arousal level going up so that he can accept even more stimulation before ejaculation. The closer he can get to the point of ejaculation without actual release, the better it feels."

Donna Brauer asked if any of us had noticed a secretion of clear fluid during arousal. I raised my hand and said I had. She asked me what the circumstances were. I said, "Sitting in an adult theater watching an explicit movie." My classmates laughed nervously. Donna Brauer asked me delicately if I touched myself at such times. I said no. "Then you're lucky," she said.

To me these discoveries and technologies were revelations. What the Brauers called male ESO (for "extended sexual orgasm") I was already doing, more or less. Female ESO might be a way to realize my central fantasy of a woman fully aroused. At the end of the afternoon I rushed to the podium and identified myself to the Brauers as a writer, which momentarily nonplussed them. "Have you written about this?" I asked them. Alan Brauer blushed. "Not yet," he said, embarrassed. "We've been so busy we haven't had time."

With an enthusiast's zeal I told him that what they'd described was revolutionary, as if they didn't know.

"We plan to write it up," he said defensively. "We're working on getting EEG measurements first."

"You ought to," I told him. "If you don't, someone else will." I didn't realize until later that Brauer thought I was talking about a scientific paper. I wasn't. I was talking about a popular book.

It hit me on the way to the airport. ESO was something everyone ought to know about. I'd been working on *The Making of the Atomic Bomb* for two years. I had three more years of research and writing to do. My two children had just started college. I'd been wondering where to turn for support. Here, dropped into my lap, was a project that shouldn't take more than six months to carry through. By one estimate, as many as half the marriages in the United States were sexually dysfunctional. A training manual would alleviate some of that pain. *The Joy of Sex*, a breezy tone poem eroticized with softcore drawings, had sold some 25 million copies. Solid information about how to improve and even extend orgasm ought to do at least as well. All I had to do was to convince the Brauers that they needed a ghost.

I gave them time to return to Palo Alto—a couple of days. Then I called them. Alan sounded suspicious. I had to repeat two or three times that working together on a book wouldn't cost him anything. I'd carry my own expenses and recover them from any advance we earned. I told him I'd like to come out to Palo Alto and talk the project over. He conferred with his wife and they agreed.

They needed convincing. They weren't sure they were ready. We talked across a long dinner. I explained how books are done—a proposal which we'd circulate through my agent, an advance from a publisher. Then I'd come out and we'd tape the book—essentially their weekend seminar, which they knew by heart. I'd have the tapes transcribed, turn speech into prose. They'd review the draft, I'd fix it, we'd send it in.

How had they discovered extended orgasm? I asked

them. They were vague about the circumstances. They learned it from the couple in the video, they said, from Susan and Marc. Alan said he'd returned to his clinic (where he and Donna treated all sorts of problems—stress, smoking, obesity, intractable pain) so excited about what he'd learned that he'd offered to teach patients who came in with other agendas. They bolted for the door, he said. The Brauers realized then that they needed to find ways to introduce people to sexual enhancement gradually. The training program they devised was their own, adapted from behavioral-modification therapies. That was their contribution: a program that gradually advanced from basic exercises in communication and intimacy to training in extending orgasm. "Over there across the bay," Alan said obscurely, "they just drop people into the middle of it. I've seen people panic and run all the way back to New York because of an experience like that. Most people can't handle that much exposure. It's too overwhelming all at once."

A few weeks later we signed a letter of agreement and went about the business of preparing a proposal. My agent submitted it to my own publisher first. "Not our sort of book," the word came back across a weekend. An editor at another house, a woman, sniffed that ESO sounded like old stuff, Tantric yoga.

I couldn't imagine that anyone who heard about ESO wouldn't immediately want to learn it. I told people about it. Their reactions amazed me. Women expressed much more interest than men. Intellectuals were the worst. They either wrote off the Brauers' claims as fraudulent or labeled such sexual enlightenment vulgar, destructive, intrusive, unspontaneous, unromantic or crude. Masters and Johnson had been dismissed the same way, and Kinsey before them, their work savagely attacked. On the other hand, my gay barber and the black woman who cleaned my house were eager to buy a copy.

Eventually my agent found a publisher, Warner Books, which took hard- and softcover rights together for $75,000. After the agent's 10 percent fee and the split with the Brauers I would earn $33,750, one-third on signing the contract, one-third on delivering the manuscript, the final third on publication. With college bills running above $20,000 annually I was bitterly disappointed. The truth is, $75,000 wasn't a bad advance in 1981 for a four-page outline from an unknown team of California sex therapists and a writer whose books hadn't sold all that well.

Working with the Brauers was easy at first. They lived in a spacious redwood house high in the hills above Portola Valley, outside Palo Alto, where eucalyptus trees scented the air. I went out one weekend and taped the book in two marathon twelve-hour days. I watched the thirty-minute orgasm demonstration again. I watched a video the Brauers had made of male ESO training. It wasn't a success. The man's partner stimulated him manually for thirty minutes, pausing from time to time to lave on lubricant, but perhaps because the camera was running, he never appeared exceptionally aroused. It was like watching someone churn butter.

I learned more about the parallels between my personal sexual discoveries and the discoveries that the Brauers had unearthed. I hadn't realized that male orgasm had been characterized as a two-stage process, but I'd been exploring plateau-phase orgasm in masturbation for years. I used a lubricant, which most men don't. ("Most men aren't into marathon masturbation, Dick," Alan told me impatiently when I wondered aloud why.) I'd learned that stimulation sustained over a long period of time built higher and higher levels of arousal. I'd learned to move as close as possible to ejaculatory urgency without cresting over into ejaculation, though I'd tended to peak myself rather than try to stay there. I'd discovered the area the Brauers called the "external prostate spot," the perineum, where rhythmic pressure mimics the pulses of orgasm.

Back home I had the interview tapes transcribed. From them I drafted a clear, straightforward text. I came to think of it as the sex manual I'd have wanted to give my children when they came of age. It began with basic anatomy, emphasized loving concern between partners and culminated in training for ESO. The Brauers and I shipped the manuscript back and forth making changes. They would lard it with what I thought of as California psychobabble and I would trim it back to standard English. Donna made sure it didn't neglect what she called romance—the delicate social foreplay of phone calls and flowers and dinners by candlelight. At some point we declared a truce and turned the manuscript in. It was all information and technique; our editor at Warner asked for stories, case studies, which the Brauers supplied. Warner accepted the revised manuscript.

Then we had to come up with illustrations, at our own expense. We agreed we didn't want to use photographs. They'd be unacceptably explicit. I wanted drawings at least as tender and erotically arousing as the drawings in *The Joy of Sex*. Alex Comfort's text was dense and quirky; I was convinced his book had sold on the strength of its illustrations, to middle-class buyers too inhibited to buy bare pornography. Our illustrations would be functional, not decorative, but making them tastefully erotic wouldn't hurt. I lived at that time in Kansas City, Missouri, where Hallmark Cards employs some four hundred artists—the company likes to claim it operates the largest art studio in the world. I proposed to find an artist there for *ESO*. My editor wouldn't hear of it. He didn't believe that Kansas City fielded artists at least as skillful as those he could find in Manhattan and considerably less expensive. I should have stuck by my guns. The artist Warner eventually hired had an uncertain grasp of anatomy. When he drew a man's leg passing behind a woman's body it sometimes reappeared offset a full diameter.

He wanted photographs to draw from. The Brauers delivered a stack of dark Polaroid close-ups demonstrating such techniques as two-handed clitoral stimulation, scrotal traction and the double-ring stretch stroke. If the photographs hadn't been produced for legitimate medical purposes, any jury in the land would have judged them obscene.

The artist raised the ante. Inserts weren't enough, he complained; he needed full-body photographs of models.

Alan and I chewed over the problem by phone. We decided that he and Donna would supply Polaroids of a couple assuming the proper positions and I would use them to pose a pair of professional models for black-and-white eight-by-tens.

I knew a local fashion photographer who dreamed of selling centerfolds. I told him my problem. He'd worked with a couple, both part-time models, who'd posed for him in the nude. He'd see about hiring them. We'll have an artist change the faces, I told him, so that no one will recognize them. We'll make them Ken and Barbie (we did).

The models were willing. We decided to shoot all twelve photographs in one long session, at night.

The woman was slim and small-breasted, the man stocky and muscular, with curly hair. I brought along a bottle of wine and an assortment of gourmet box lunches that encouraged them to believe I meant them no harm.

We agreed they'd pose wearing bikini bottoms, the woman topless. (The photographer told me he could probably convince the couple to perform on camera, not merely to pose. That made my ears buzz, but as soon as he whispered the offer I realized I couldn't possibly teach two strangers the full battery of ESO techniques on the spot. Warner was pushing to get the illustrations. So I missed becoming a pornographer by the breadth of a deadline.)

We needed a *faux* erection. I'd browsed a dime store that afternoon, looking for something suitable. I considered hair curlers, dowel rods and toilet-paper rollers before I realized that a candle would work. I walked to a nearby Hallmark shop. Hallmark scents most of its candles with perfumes so intense they make my head ache, but among the few unscented candles in the store display I spotted one brave yellow cylinder that might serve. It was a little on the hefty side, six inches long and two inches in diameter—John Holmes in 50 percent reduction. When I produced it at the beginning of the photography session it broke what was left of the ice.

I spent the evening wading among pillows and satin sheets in my stocking feet arranging body parts—the author at work. I'd wondered how I'd handle so intimate an experience. I handled it fine. I switched effortlessly into the warm professionalism I'd learned as a surgical assistant in the Air Force, when I'd had to manage such delicate assignments as shaving a fellow airman's testicles with a dry straight razor (you hold the penis aside firmly with a gauze sponge and talk about sports). The models, who after all were lovers, enjoyed themselves. Late in the session I noticed that the woman had lubricated enough to wet the crotch of her bikini. The photographer developed the film and printed a set of contact sheets the same evening to make sure everything came out; when the woman noticed her crotch was wet she hooted with surprise.

ESO, subtitled *The New Promise of Pleasure for Couples in Love* and *How You and Your Lover Can Give Each Other Hours of Extended Sexual Orgasm*, was published in somewhat shabby hardcover—paper over boards—in 1983. Warner's timing was awful or diabolical; the other sex book of the season, *The G-Spot*, appeared one month later and swept the field. Hardly anyone reviewed our much more comprehensive and revolutionary text, certainly not *The New York Times*. Warner believed too loyally in the book's intrinsic appeal to eclipse it with advertising. We had the good luck to sell book club rights to the Literary Guild, which featured the book with a photograph of an attractive man and woman nude in each other's arms and carried it lucratively on its backlist for the next three years. But *ESO* started slowly, and my vision that it might rocket to the upper ranks of the best-seller list and stay there forever, like *The Joy of Sex*, gave way to the reality that the book was too explicit in subject and in illustration— two drawings demonstrated fellatio and cunnilingus—for open store display. Bookstores bought it and then proceeded to bury it deep in their Psychology or Health shelves, spine out.

I introduced it that year as a panel-discussion topic at the annual free-for-all known as the World Affairs Conference in Boulder, Colorado. The description I'd written for the conference catalog drew a crowd of young women who jammed the discussion room to the walls. The other panel members included two sociologists, husband and wife, a woman who was an expatriate Russian poet and the film critic Roger Ebert. The Russian poet dismissed the book (which she hadn't read) impatiently; she said she thought the American preoccupation with sexual athleticism vulgarized love. The husband sociologist indicted the book as a potential menace to the family. Parents would like pleasuring each other so much, he speculated bizarrely, that they'd neglect their children. Three or four hours in the bedroom every afternoon, what would the children do? The women in the audience chewed him up and spat him out. Roger Ebert offered a brief but charming review, as if the book were a little movie. He emphasized its Yankee-craftsman approach. He said he especially liked the section that cautioned lovers to bathe carefully and keep their fingernails trimmed for manual stimulation. *ESO*, he said, coining a phrase, was an American *Kama Sutra*.

The book did eventually succeed commercially, almost entirely by word of mouth, and my children got through college. Warner issued *ESO* in paperback in 1984. For several years thereafter it jogged along steadily at about five hundred copies a month. Then, as if our readership had achieved some critical mass, royalties began to increase from one six-month reporting period to the next. They're still increasing, with more than two hundred thousand copies in print. The Dutch, the Hungarians, the Australians, the Poles and the Czechs have bought rights, but not the French, the British or the Japanese.

We included a brief survey questionnaire at the end of the book that readers could answer and send in. Hundreds of completed surveys and personal letters arrived in Palo Alto. People reported good results—not necessarily extended orgasm, but improved communication, more pleasure and rejuvenated relationships. The Brauers were relieved; the medical community had criticized them for raising expectations too high. A doctor I knew socially whispered to me in his office one morning that the book had saved his marriage. Another acquaintance, a teacher, whispered the same grateful confession.

An old friend from college who's now a private detective filled in the rest of the story for me. He noticed an article in *Oui* magazine about More University, a Lafayette, California, degree-granting institution devoted to advanced sex education, that opened with a description of the video the Brauers use in their seminars. More University, it seemed, produced it and sells it; it's called "How to Do a Woman." A man named Victor Baranco founded More. My friend checked him out. Baranco's was the off-camera voice directing the video. Susan was Baranco's ex-wife. Marc was More's medical director. Baranco makes a cameo appearance in Gay Talese's 1980 book *Thy Neighbor's Wife* in a chronicle of "alternative-life-style communities" (i.e., communes):

> Within a secluded residence in the woodlands of Lafayette, a suburb of Oakland, lived a thirty-four-year-old advocate of "responsible hedonism" named Victor Baranco, who, having made money in real-estate developing, now had several mini-communes throughout California and in other states; and *Rolling Stone* magazine called Baranco "the Colonel Sanders of the commune scene."

Just as Alex Comfort had gone to Sandstone, roamed the orgies and communicated what he learned to more conventional readers in *The Joy of Sex*, so it seemed that the Brauers had gone to More University and adapted that experience for more conventional clients in their program of ESO training. In both cases reputable professionals (Comfort is a distinguished British gerontologist) transferred new knowledge from the radical fringe into the straight community, rather like botanists returning from the jungle with promising new medicinals.

I knew ESO had lodged itself permanently in the American psyche when I opened the *New York Review of Books* for May 8, 1986, and found the following Personals ad:

SEEK ESO PARTNER WM M.D. seeks serious attractive youngish female for the [sic] study and mutual training in the [sic] Extended Sexual Orgasm as described in Dr. Alan Brauer's book on the subject. No professionals. Box 239. . . .

Two hundred thousand copies. How many readers? Four hundred thousand? Six hundred thousand? How many people have at least heard about the possibility of intensifying sexual pleasure, of adding that gift to their lives, because I happened to open a catalog one morning? What else don't we know? What else might we learn if we talked to one another?

I Heard G——'s Lovely Voice . . .

I heard G——'s lovely voice for the first time when she left a message on my answering machine. She said she was the producer of a talk show and wondered if I'd be a guest. She left her name and number. I called her back. I knew her host; he'd interviewed me several times before. I said I'd be glad to do the show and we set a date.

It's impossible to guess someone's appearance from her voice if her voice is trained, as G——'s is. G—— was smaller than I'd expected. I walked into the sound studio and glimpsed clavicles and small shoulders, tanned, high cheekbones and curly chestnut hair. The scoop-necked, loosely woven linen sweater G—— was wearing over a khaki skirt revealed the lift and separation of her breasts. I had to ignore her for her smiling host long enough to recover. As I sat down to start the show she asked me if I needed anything. I said I could use a cup of water. She breezed out of the room and returned with a coffee carafe of water and a ceramic mug. "We pour our own drinks around here," she warned. I felt her eyes on my back for the duration of the show. I wanted to turn and smile at her, but it wasn't clear if she would return my smile or frown at me for presuming. Afterward I found I'd visualized her sweater as chain mail and wondered why. Because G—— had been brisk and direct, I realized, friendly but also guarded. If she was slim and small, she was also physically intense. She could have been a dancer or a student of karate. It turned out she was both.

I thought about G—— through the next week as I went about my work. It seemed to me we'd struck some resonance between us. It took my breath away. I wondered if she'd sensed it as well. I decided I wanted to see her again, wanted to know more about her, wanted to make love with her.

I was married at the time, but for several years I'd felt my marriage drifting. It was my second marriage, the two together totaling nearly twenty-five years of commitment. I was forty-nine years old, looking to the last third of my life, and I no longer believed that I should honor marriage before personal happiness. I didn't think I wanted a divorce. I thought I wanted a second relationship, a more intensely sexual relationship, and imagined that opening the marriage in that way might somehow improve it. My wife and I had already talked it over in general terms. Reluctantly she'd agreed.

So calling G—— committed me to moving away from the security of convention. It felt like diving off a headland into an uncertain sea. I searched for a plausible reason to invite G—— to lunch. The thought of what I was about to do made my throat dry and my voice thin—tension I'd suffered from for years in the first few minutes at least of public appearances. I saw that my throttled voice could serve a useful purpose for once. I waited until a comfortable morning and called.

I'd asked G—— to send me a tape of the show. As soon as I identified myself on the phone she said, "I've-got-your-tape-on-my-desk-I-just-haven't-sent-it-yet." I said, "Oh, that's all right, send it whenever you can." And abruptly we both hung up.

I stared at my desk, stricken. G——'s defensiveness had completely thrown me off. Was my adventure over before it had even begun? I wondered what to do next. It took me a few minutes to realize that all I had to do was pick up the phone, call G—— back and try again.

I did. "You were so quick about the tape I forgot to say why I called," I told G——. "I didn't call about the tape. I called because I have a problem that I'd like your advice about."

"A problem?" G—— repeated uncertainly.

Don't go into it now, I cautioned myself; as efficient as this woman seems to be, she might solve it on the phone. "I think it's something you can help me with," I hurried on. "It comes up in public speaking. I wonder if you'd like to have lunch? I could explain better then."

She said she would. We made a date. I put down the phone and found my heart beating wildly, a grin on my face.

The day came and I was nervous. I picked up G—— at the radio station and drove to a restaurant I'd chosen nearby. It was a Middle Eastern restaurant and the service was usually disorganized but the food was good. I parked and we walked half a block in the summer heat only to discover a crowd at the door waiting for seating. I nearly panicked. Where could we go? I apologized profusely for making G—— walk. She shrugged it off: she didn't mind. We got back in the car and drove ten minutes south to another restaurant I knew in a shopping center. It wasn't crowded. The hostess seated us immediately. My panic faded and we settled in to talk.

How much did I learn about G—— that day? It's hard to remember now. That her people came from southwestern Missouri, old English stock, as mine did? That her cheekbones were Cherokee? I liked her bright, alert eyes, their hazel irises flecked with green and gold. I liked her open smile. She had an overbite. I hadn't noticed it before. I liked that too and found it sexy. She was informed and impatient. She understood irony. She was smart.

We got my ostensible problem out of the way, since it puzzled her. I told her about my voice. She gave me the name of her voice teacher but cautioned me that training was long and hard. She mentioned warm-up exercises and sounds, lemon water. We talked about our work. We talked about books and writing.

I'd thought about what next. I'd just begun research on a book about a farm family. Driving back and forth from the farm, an hour and a half east of the city, I passed a park on a bluff overlooking the Missouri River that surrounded an antebellum house restored as a museum. I told G—— about it. It was a lovely place for a picnic, I said. Would she like to go on a picnic there with me? She would. We made a date. I drove her back to the radio station and dropped her off. I watched her walk inside, an intense, self-possessed woman in her early thirties with a rich voice and chestnut curls. Her head came up to my shoulder. I outweighed her by at least eighty pounds. She was completely different physically from any woman I'd ever pursued before. The two women I'd married were physically similar—taller, darker, heavier—a pattern I'd taken for an imprint. I didn't know if G——'s difference from the pattern was promising or not.

I wanted to spread the picnic on a gingham cloth. I looked in a kitchen store, a dime store and a department store; no one seemed to carry gingham. Finally I went to a fabric store. When I told the manager what I needed and why, she was charmed. She had blue plaid damask; for twenty-five dollars I bought a picnic spread of that. The morning of the picnic I made sandwiches of smoked turkey on French rolls and packed cold artichokes and strawberries.

I went about these preparations dazed, pleasantly tingling, a little short of breath. They were simple and physical, anchored in the real, yet they portended revelations, enlarging mysteries, intimacy, the possibility of both ecstasy and great pain. I'd been feeling numbed, buried, and now already felt ardently naked and exposed. Packing a picnic, choosing the clothes I would wear, I was preparing to reveal myself body and soul to another human being who had accepted my invitation for a second meeting knowing that I was married and who might therefore be preparing to reveal herself body and soul to me.

We found a place on a dogleg of the park that was nearly private, where the grass sloped toward the bluff and we could watch the wide brown river. I'd put so much turkey in the sandwiches it squeezed out when we bit into them. A safari of ants wandered by. We sat through a misty drizzle, which gave me occasion to tell G—— about making love once outdoors beside an antiaircraft missile battery in a warm rain—the night long ago with R——. Then the sun broke through and the air steamed and it was Missouri summer again, midafternoon, time for me to declare myself. I was suddenly so nervous that G—— complained I was making her nervous as well and asked me to calm down. I swallowed hard, looked in her eyes and told her that I thought she was lovely and that I'd like to make love with her. We could stop at a motel on the way back, I said.

We both blushed. G—— hesitated, working it out. "I have to be back at four," she told me. "I'd rather wait," she started, and I was despondent. But she continued, "Until we have enough time," adding "I don't like to rush," and I was jubilant. Driving back to the city I reached across the gearbox and took her hand. We turned to look at each other and smiled our alliance. I understood that G—— was glad she'd come, and that the next time we met we'd make love.

I scouted a place. Somewhere east of the city where I wasn't likely to encounter anyone I knew. Though I'd never told my partners everything I thought, I'd tried to be forthright about what I did. Now I was moving to limit that candor so that I wouldn't have to manage rapid change in two relationships at the same time. My wife had consented in the abstract to opening our marriage; I doubted if she would accept the reality. I was afraid that the conflict that would probably result would distort and finally deform my fragile new link with G——. I didn't see—perhaps I didn't want to see—that by favoring the new over the existing relationship I had already begun to choose between them.

The place I found was a major hotel northeast across the river, not far off my usual route to the farm where I was working four and sometimes five days a week. G—— wouldn't have to drive more than twenty minutes each way. I checked and learned that the hotel offered a day rate if the room was vacated by five. I called G—— and invited her to meet me. She agreed and I reserved a room.

The day of our meeting G—— called up from the lobby. I waited for her at the elevator and we walked back together to the room, a sunny room with two double beds and a view of the green to the south behind the hotel. We had the afternoon to share in absolute privacy. No one knew our whereabouts. G—— and I were preparing to invent a new culture of private speech and touch and gesture, a new human world, just as I did when I wrote fiction. Lifted out of the known world, I felt free to improvise.

We ordered lunch and ate it at the table at the window with the gauze drapes pulled against the sun. I don't remember what we talked about. Our lives, I suppose. "Ah, the story," as my private-detective friend says: sooner or later people always tell their stories. G—— and I probably told each other our stories that afternoon, the abridged versions, the versions everyone tells first. I'm sure we filled the space of privacy we'd made together with something more than small talk. The mute, abundant beds there like an audience listening would have prompted us to candor.

We'd already begun, sharing a meal, but how did we decide to begin? Eventually the pattern becomes familiar; at the beginning you have to think it through. One of us might have raised an eyebrow: "Well?" I'm sure both of us smiled then, nodded and pushed back our chairs. Then a chasm to cross, the wide, terrific gulf between image and body, between the virtual and the real. We crossed it running across the air: holding our breaths, composing our faces expectantly, standing, coming together, raising our arms to embrace. Catching each other before we fell, our entire bodies sighing.

We discovered that we kissed with our eyes open, like curious children. It was strange bending down so far to kiss, G——'s face looking up, her lips gentle, strange to feel G—— standing on tiptoe, to hold someone so small. She wasn't fragile. She was lean and strong. The muscles of her shoulders and her back had definition. She'd told me that part of her story by now, that she'd studied ballet and still danced once a week, that for a year she'd been taking karate.

Hand in hand to the far bed, away from the window,

and we lay down together fully dressed (she was wearing a red sweater and a linen skirt; the afternoon, she remembers, wrecked the skirt). We opened our mouths to each other. I searched her mouth with my tongue, but she also searched mine. We flicked the tips of our tongues, a tremor that augmented through our bodies. I slipped my hand to G——'s breast and she covered it with her own. I slipped my hand outside her skirt to cup her *mons* and she reached in turn to cup the swell of my erection. So we wrote on each other's bodies how we proposed to make love. I read that G—— would not be passive.

We undressed each other. At other times with other women I'd found that operation awkward; with G—— it was exciting, an unveiling and a gift. I took her in all at once: willowy, pale where she'd worn a bikini, small crescent breasts, surprising child's light pink nipples, brown moles flecking her shoulders and her chest, a flat belly brushed with down suspended between the points of her hips, brown, soft pubic hair, strong legs. When she turned on her side to face me and brought her leg over my waist, her small, tight buttock made a hollow where it inserted at her thigh. She might have been a photographer's model for the anatomy her body revealed. Her skin was resilient, smooth and warm—a woman's flesh under a child's fine surface.

Desire made me hollow. I wanted to drink her. I turned her on her back. She was willing; she watched me with wide eyes. I slid off the end of the bed to kneel on the floor and drew her hips near the edge, feeling her femurs pivoting. She raised her knees and pliéd. A nest, delicate small wings. I slipped my hands under her buttocks, like raising a deep, refreshing bowl. I brought my face to her and licked open her labia.

Inside she was rose-pink, the same delicate rose as her

lips. Her taste was delicate as well, without musk, a child's breath.

She gasped. She rotated up to press my mouth, her buttocks clenching. The tip of my tongue found the small bud of her clitoris. I fed in saliva and flicked. The tongue magnifies; searching up and under her clitoral hood was like searching the arch of a doorway. Tenting the arch gave her clitoris the softer tissue on the underside of my tongue but also the strum of frenulum there. I looked across her belly to watch; she quivered to it and clutched at her breast.

I saw that she might come to my mouth. I anchored the tip of my tongue under the arch of her hood and turned my head from side to side, substituting pressure for movement so that my blind tongue wouldn't lose its place. Even my tongue felt coarse against that distended bulb of tissue and I fed in saliva to slick us. She was stirring, flexing, her buttocks working in my hands, her battered dancer's feet pressing into the bed beside my shoulders to anchor her. I was too busy to look up but I heard her voicing, not loud, an "ah! Ah! AH!" steepening in pitch, and then with no more warning her body fired explosively, every muscle contracting, and her back arched *grand mal* off the bed from the abutments of her feet and her shoulders. Sounding her climax, her voice curved over its range like the arch her back made. I didn't know how far her pleasure might go; I kept my tongue anchored and my head turning until she groped for my hair and pushed me away.

I climbed up quickly beside her. She was still adrift and I watched her identity return.

I wanted urgently to enter her. I'd brought condoms, lambskins. I found a package and fumbled to break the seal and pulled one on. I shifted between G——'s legs. In recent years, with others, the first time had been awkward; I'd had trouble maintaining an erection. With G—— I was erect and straining, a pulse at my throat, a tremor of excitement in my hands. I asked her to put me in. She notched me and I entered her. She was wet, and I went in easily, but it was my turn to gasp. We fit tightly; like the rest of her muscles, her internal muscles were toned. On my elbows above her I began to move, reading my own arousal to pace myself, my turn. I felt as if a hand were holding me, as if I were being milked; her vagina resisted when I thrust and pulled when I withdrew. We studied each other's faces. That was new as well, that frankness. I saw a woman who wished me pleasure curious at my response and marveled that while we examined each other so openly, as if across a table by candlelight, our bodies coupled below, our genitals slipped and scalded.

It was exquisite to make love with someone so small and light, the acromions of her shoulders to grasp, leaning aside to cup her small breasts, stroking her flat stomach, the taut indentures of her buttocks strapping my belly when she lifted her legs to embed me. I felt as if we were a boy and a girl. Waves of pleasure silted my awareness and we became boy and girl, pubescent. Far off in a hotel room, fading, a middle-aged man saw that the woman making love with him would rescue in him the innocent sensuality of the childhood he had missed. Oh and then I was gone, bellowing, all of me rushing down and across that rigid lumen, bursting through the boundary wall between us as a spring bursts.

The room returned. I stroked more slowly, eking out the attenuating pulse until it faded. I'd held myself up on my elbows so G—— could see my face in orgasm, to show her how much pleasure she gave me. I opened my eyes and saw that she had watched.

We talked away what was left of the afternoon, lying nude together, touching each other, adding something of our sexual histories to our stories. I learned that I was the first man to bring G—— to orgasm with his mouth. I told her about ESO, that it was a good way to get to know each other sexually. She was eager to learn; I arranged to drop off a copy of the book. We washed, dressed, embraced and went our ways, she to her evening talk show, I to the motel where I was staying during the week while I worked on the farm.

We met when we could after that sweet beginning— at best, one afternoon a week for the next several months, usually at the hotel. My paranoia about being seen in public abated and we had lunch in the restaurant before we went to our dayroom upstairs. We kissed and held each other in welcome, then undressed, washed our genitals and slipped into bed. Naked in each other's arms we continued kissing and holding each other until we focused our lives within the field of that quiet room. I liked kissing G——, liked the delicacy of her lips and her active tongue, her dancing eyes full of mischief, liked holding her shoulders and strok- ing her back, sweeping the palm of my hand down into the small of her back and then up and over her tight buttocks, cupping her buttocks one at a time and working the line of my fingers into their warm cleft.

We almost always began our lovemaking with cunnilin- gus. G—— liked it and so did I. Since she seldom mas- turbated, by the time we met on those stolen afternoons she hadn't had sex for a week or more; my slightest touch on her vulva made her buzz. Following the ESO canon, I encouraged her to vocalize in lovemaking. (It's distracting to think about keeping quiet; vocalizing is another way to let go.) G—— went full-throated, as I had already learned to do. She found it easy to sound her feelings; her voice exercises may have prepared her.

I licked inside her pubic hair. She had *labia minora*

like small pale wings, one longer than the other and over-lapping. I sucked one and then the other into my mouth and gently tugged it, which made her moan but also laugh, a clear, sparkling laugh of pleasure like a happy child's. Eventually I told her she was my angel, an angel sent to me as a gift of grace in the last half of my life, and the delicate wings of her *labia minora* I called her angel wings. "They sent you to earth in disguise," I told her, making up a children's story and repeating it from week to week for our childish pleasure in hearing it repeated. "The devil can't disguise both his cloven hoofs at the same time, so if you watch closely you see him switching a hoof from one foot to the other so fast it's almost a blur, and you angels can't completely disguise your wings, so you hide yours down between your legs. But I found you out." I'd finish by sucking one of those warm wings into my mouth and playing it with my tongue. G—— would laugh her delicious laugh and I'd feel as if the story I'd just made up might well be true.

Or I told her a cautionary tale of the Hottentot apron, a cosmetic deformity that I'd encountered in an obscure nineteenth-century French African medical narrative doc-umented with an engraving. Mothers deliberately stretched their daughters' *labia minora*, beginning in child-hood, until by adolescence they hung like apron flaps down halfway to the knees, the better to clasp the Hottentot husband's penis. G—— would widen her eyes in mock horror, playing along, but once or twice she asked me se-riously if she needed to worry about her labia lengthening. "Only when you're hot," I told her. Did I only imagine that I could feel her wings fluttering at the base of my penis when I thrust deep inside her?

At that first intense orgasm under my tongue the veins in her neck bulged, she clutched her breasts, her face went red, she arched and roared. Incredible and beautiful that so small an area of the body's surface should trigger such an explosion of pleasure. I moved up beside G—— while she recovered. I'd noticed the first time we made love, and I noticed again for the first weeks thereafter, that even in her daze of postorgasmic bliss she was careful not to put her head on my shoulder; unapproachably she held herself apart. A few weeks along, without warning, she turned to me and nestled. I waited until she was fully conscious and told her I'd noticed. She hadn't realized. She thought it over. "It means I trust you," she said finally. "I've never let anyone in this way before." I drew her closer. Then a second gift, her tears dropping warm onto my chest. I turned up her face; tears welled from wide eyes that she wasn't ashamed to let me see, tears of release. "I never cry, either," she told me wryly. "I never cry and I never let anyone in." She laughed, but the laugh broke over into weeping. Neither of us was ready yet to say I love you. I held her. My eyes filled with tears. I told her she was beautiful. I told her she was safe with me, safe in my arms. I meant it, as much as I could mean it when I didn't know where my own safety lay.

G—— had been on her own since she was sixteen, when she'd walked away from a childhood of cruelty and neglect that began when the father she no longer consciously remembered had murdered her infant brother in her presence in a fit of rage. She'd always been competent, taking care of herself and her younger sisters; she'd learned to be tough. She had an abortion at eighteen, alone. She'd been fifty pounds overweight as a teenager; in her twenties she fought her weight down to willowy strength and kept it there. She put herself through college—eleven years of night school before she finally got her degree. She worked her way up from bartending and waitressing to become manager of convention operations for a major hotel. She decided she'd die young of drugs and drink if she kept that job. She quit, went through voice training and lived on peanut butter in a cockroach-infested apartment while she worked for the radio station without pay for six months until the station manager saw her abilities and hired her. She still smoked, but she was preparing to stop. She didn't tell me much about the men in her life. She'd been deeply in love only once, to a man who'd seemed to want her but then had pushed her away when she came too close.

All those years, alone out somewhere beyond the edge of the world, she'd guarded within herself the lovely, expressive child she'd had to hide away in childhood to protect from violation. Allowing me to comfort her in that vulnerable moment after orgasm was an extraordinary gift, an intimation that she felt safe enough with me to permit that child release.

My childhood had begun with a murder as well—my mother's violent suicide—and like G——, I had grown up expectant. It will always be a mystery to me how we found each other, how we recognized our convergence before we knew the facts. I'd fallen in love before, many times, instantly and narcotically, and then tried to make the best of a relationship when the narcotic wore off. What was happening with G—— wasn't falling in love, not the same way. It was deeper than that. It was more like finding a long-lost twin, G——'s indomitable child and mine, sensing that they might have room to heal and play and grow in the space of privacy we could make together, joining together to protect them. The first strong emotion I felt for G—— after desire was respect. For her courage. For having survived with her capacity to love intact. And following from respect, gratitude, for offering that generous spirit to me so soon and so guilelessly, her head on my shoulder, her uninhibited passion in my arms.

I'd never met anyone so comfortable with her sexuality before. G—— had never met anyone so interested in her response. She walked around unself-consciously nude and lay beside me with her knees raised and open, offering her vulva comfortably to my view. The second time we met for lovemaking I brought along a jar of Albolene, a less viscous alternative to Vaseline that the Brauers recommend for sexual lubrication. After cunnilingus I lubricated G——'s vulva with Albolene and caressed her to one or two more orgasms before I even thought of joining in. She liked me to slide her clitoris between my index and middle fingers, a touch she normally used herself, but as she pulsed near climax I learned to stroke the bud of her clitoris lightly with the pad of my third finger. That teasing drove her crazy; she came explosively and I could almost immediately begin again.

If I had once, as an adolescent, managed seven ejaculations in one day, now in middle age I could at best manage three, and usually no more than two. Peaking myself in first-stage orgasm more than compensated for that natural diminution. I'd learned to peak myself self-stimulating; it was easy to transfer that skill to intercourse. After G——'s first two or three orgasms on our afternoons of lovemaking I entered her from above or lay back so she could ride me. Early in the relationship I controlled our movements. She soon found ways to answer my stroking with her own. On her back, she raised her legs to rock her pelvis as I thrust, which ran the ring of muscle inside the entrance to her vagina back and forth across my frenulum and sent me almost instantly peaking. Riding me, she bowed and arched her back, ringing my frenulum the same way from above, a motion that added the visual pleasure of watching her buttocks perk as their curve drew more acute.

For a variation, because her small vagina clasped me so tightly, I held myself over her on my hands and knees so that the only part of my body that touched her was my penis sliding along her vaginal wall. I could do that only briefly; despite the controls I'd learned I found the sensation—and the idea of it, its elaboration in fantasy—overwhelming; I'd have to stop unless I wanted to ejaculate.

Fortunately for my controls we had to stop frequently anyway so G—— could pee. As many women do until they're well advanced in arousal, she read the stroking of my penis or finger against her upper vaginal wall as a bladder signal. It distracted her. During our first few afternoons together I thought she wasn't paying attention. Since increasing pleasure requires two people working together on one person's arousal, we came close to arguing about it. But each time it happened it turned out to be her bladder. I learned to recognize it, sometimes even earlier than she did. "Do you have to pee?" I'd ask her, stopping stroking. She'd think for a moment. "Yes. You're right. I do." We called it the metaphysics of the bladder, a problem of the body that masqueraded as a problem with the relationship.

Taking my turn, I peaked myself half a dozen times across fifteen or twenty minutes, each time moving to a higher level of arousal, a little closer to the edge, stopping stroking a little sooner until I didn't dare move at all. When simply pulsing my penis inside her or G—— pulsing around me was enough to risk ejaculation, I withdrew and went back to pleasuring her. Kneeling at her side I slicked her with Albolene, held her labia open with my left hand and retracted her clitoral hood. Fully engorged, a miniature almond plump and oval where it disappeared into its hood, erecting almost to a point, her clitoris shone translucently rose. I stroked it lightly with the index finger of my right hand, catching only the very tip, sensation so intense that G——'s hands hovered over mine, barely resisting pushing mine away. She wasn't long coming. Her eyelids fluttered, the whites showed as her eyes rolled up, her head jerked back, her feet flexed down, her moan loudened to a roar and she arched in convulsion in her powerful last orgasm of the afternoon. I followed, wearing a condom, thrusting deep inside her, aware of her slim strong arms around me and the taut straps of her adductors at the back of her raised thighs until awareness overflowed and I dispersed into the flood.

In late September I rented an apartment in a small town near the farm where I was working. A farmer who'd lost his farm in the rural crash of the early Reagan years had bought a grade-school building and converted it to apartments. It still looked like a school, schoolroom doors with frosted glass in their upper panels opening off a wide concrete-floored hall. For seventy-five dollars a month I rented a single room up a flight of stairs at the end of the hall, under the roof. It must have been the principal's office once. It wasn't more than twelve by twelve, but it had a single window, a kitchen and a bathroom with a shower. A wooden ledge along the west wall narrow as a crib made a shelf for a bed.

I drove to the farm on Monday morning, stayed at my small studio Monday and Tuesday nights, drove home Wednesday afternoon, came back to the studio Thursday night and went home again at the end of the day on Friday. That opened a free Thursday afternoon. G—— and I began meeting at her apartment in the city before I drove out to the country. I brought gourmet box lunches that we ate at her round dining table in the alcove outside her bedroom, her water bed waiting beyond the open door. The water bed anchored her hips; when we made love on it I felt as if I were plunging into the solid earth. She had two cats, old friends she'd raised from kittens, which sometimes watched us until boredom set in and they napped. She asked me if it bothered me that they watched. It had made one of her boyfriends uncomfortable; he'd had trouble keeping his erection. I told her I liked her cats, which I did, liked them watching. They reminded me that the room where we lay naked together was a provincial outpost of Eden, as much of Eden as we would ever know.

G—— was working hard that fall at karate, preparing to test for her orange belt at a *dojo* crowded with beefy cops and black boxers. Her *sensei* was a demon for exercise. He had his initiates building toward two hundred pushups. G—— staggered home from class; when we talked on the phone from the country to the city later in the evening I could hear the exhaustion in her voice. She lost weight. She was already slim; now the cage of her ribs formed an arch above her concave belly and the lacings of muscles tightened on her back. Her clavicles stood out from her shoulders, her high cheekbones from her almost gaunt face. I noticed the weight loss even in her vagina; at her thinnest I could feel ridges along her vaginal wall with my penis that muted if she gained back so much as a pound. When we lay together caressing each other before lovemaking I felt as if I were holding and comforting a hungry child. At those times she embodied the shadow child within her that I felt responsible for, the child I wanted to nurture as I had nurtured my own children when they were small.

G—— had gone off the Pill not long before we met. She used a diaphragm. I used condoms as well. I used them at the outset because I didn't know her sexual history and didn't want to put either myself or my wife at risk. I continued using them even after I understood that both our histories made the risk of HIV infection marginal. When she'd told me about her abortion she'd said she never wanted to go through that experience again. I took her to mean she wouldn't have another abortion. Since both my children were diaphragm children, and I didn't intend to have more, I continued using condoms. It puzzled G——. "You don't have to use that," she told me one afternoon. "But what if you get pregnant?" I asked her. "Then we'll take care of it," she said. I asked her if she meant an abortion. She said she did, and from there we talked the problem out. We decided to forgo condoms. Without them my penis got red and sore. For a few weeks I assumed the problem was the sheer wear and tear of our long afternoons of lovemaking. When my penis emerged one afternoon glowing red from tip to base, like a baboon's bright member, I finally understood something else must be wrong. G—— called her gynecologist. "It's probably your spermacide," the woman told her. "A lot of people are allergic to nonoxynol-9." G—— decided to go back on the Pill and the psychedelic hue faded from my penis. We used condoms for another month, until the Pill took effect. Then we made love bare, to the exquisite slip of her natural lubrication at the beginning of an afternoon together, adding Albolene for comfort as we extended our play.

G——'s apartment was a second-floor walkup in an old building. Instead of a shower she had a clawfooted bathtub. One afternoon she closed herself into the bathroom to prepare it for us while I waited lying naked on the bed, stroking myself in anticipation. Closed doors animated the cats; large black and small gray, they took turns yowling from the bedroom side to be let in and searching under the door with a paw. When G—— opened the door to welcome me she was naked, her body glowing in the light of the candles she'd lit in the misty, windowless room. She'd filled the old bathtub with warm water and bubble bath. We slipped into it facing each other, our legs interlaced, laved each other with suds and leaned forward to kiss. After awhile I turned G—— so that she nested between my legs, her back against my chest, and with my arms around her, my hand underwater, feeling her shudder all along my body, I caressed her to a warm, peaceful orgasm. When she was alert again I lifted myself up to the edge of the tub and she took my penis into her mouth, holding it at the base with a small, strong hand while she slipped her mouth up and down. Past experience with partners who disliked fellatio still inhibited me with G——. She assured me she enjoyed drafting my penis, but I wasn't comfortable yet pursuing the pleasure beyond foreplay. I lowered myself back into the warm water and we returned to nesting together, playing her hand spray across our bodies, dissolving into a languor that the cats eventually penetrated with their inquisitive meows.

Limiting our meetings to weekly afternoons began to seem constricting. I bought an inflatable mattress and invited G—— to drive to the country and stay with me overnight in my schoolhouse apartment. She enjoyed the drive through a countryside ripe in October with corn and soybeans, the pastures along the highway still green. She arrived before I returned from the farm; I found her waiting in the quiet of my small room in the shadows of early evening. I showered and we fixed dinner together, something simple, then moved for lovemaking to the narrow ledge padded with a futon.

We kept finding new pleasures to share. She knelt over my head and covered my face with a mask of thighs and buttocks while I licked her to orgasm. She stimulated herself with one hand while she rode me until her body trembled and convulsed and her vagina throbbed around my penis.

I loved to lick her. I told her every part of her body was delicious. It was true; she was scrupulously clean and her natural odor was delicate, almost devoid of musk. I licked her ears and her eyes and her mouth. I curled my tongue into her nostrils and tasted the salt of the tears that her eyes drained there. I licked her clavicles and her small firm breasts, her armpits, out along her arms to the soft skin on the insides of her elbows, her wrists, the palms of her hands, between her fingers. Sucking her fingers one at a time into my mouth made her moan. I licked her belly with its straps of muscle dividing around her shallow navel, following them down to her *mons*. I licked her labia and her clitoris. I licked her vaginal introitus, extending my tongue as far it would go inside to taste her lubrication. I licked her perineum and her tight pink anus until she squealed her pleasure and laughed. I licked the insides of her thighs, the hollows at the back of her knees. I strummed her Achilles tendons with my tongue. I sucked her toes and licked between them. My mouth on her body, my tongue savoring her crevices was like plunging my face into a bowl of ripe summer fruits and inhaling their mingled fragrances—peaches, apples, pears. All of her was fresh. All of her was beautiful.

She licked me in return, my face, my body, down to my groin. She licked up the shaft of my penis, around the glans, down the other side, popping my testicles into her mouth one by one, lifting my scrotum by its sac delicately with one hand and licking along my perineum below. She licked and sucked my nipples and I discovered how much arousal I could find there. It was different from the arousal that genital stimulation brought, as if a different structure of nerves had been excited.

One evening after G—— had already enjoyed several orgasms at my mouth and hands I turned to licking and sucking one of her nipples. The stimulation aroused her and I kept it up. Her legs were separated; neither one of us was touching her vulva. Licking across the nipple, flicking it, seemed to work best and I concentrated on that. G—— moaned exactly as she moaned when I was stroking her clitoris. Her sighs got louder and closer together. I tried to maintain an even pace, not to seem as if I was pushing her. And then, just as if I had licked her clitoris, she came in one sweet soft sigh. We were both surprised. I'd read in Masters and Johnson that a rare few women are capable of orgasm with breast stimulation alone. G—— was one of them. We added that delicacy to our variations.

Almost every night for nearly thirty years I had drunk myself to intoxication. I'd learned to pace, and to some degree to control, my drinking; by now, at fifty, I had sequestered serious binging—drinking myself to a stupor, drinking all night—to about one night out of ten. I don't think I ever kidded myself that alcohol was good for me. I certainly never believed that it was inspiring. To the contrary, I understood that I used it to release and at the same time to control rage, to indulge in bitter self-pity, to punish my partners for the mistake of loving me, to punish myself whenever I achieved success in my life and my work. For at least the past four years—since I quit smoking for the sixth and final time and demonstrated to myself that quitting such addictions was possible—I'd been thinking seriously about giving up drinking. I didn't want to join AA. I respected AA's results but not its methods; if possible, I wanted to quit on my own. I'd found some support for my objective in a recent book, *The Natural History of Alcoholism*, which identified within the larger population of stone alcoholics a population of problem drinkers who often quit drinking in mid-life without intervention.

I was also at that time cultivating the goodwill of the farmer whose life I hoped to chronicle in a book. We worked side by side, and it was obvious to me that showing up hung over every morning wasn't going to get me through the year. He reminded me of my older brother Stanley; I felt good about being with him and wanted his respect. His own drinking was confined to a few swigs of peppermint schnapps with his brothers the night before their annual deer hunt. He told me sadly about farmers he'd known who drank themselves to death.

From the beginning I'd drunk very little around G——. It wasn't a question of willpower. We met in the afternoons and I rarely started drinking before evening. Once, when I had my house to myself, I invited G—— to spend the night. We drank wine that evening, continuing after supper, lying together in front of the fireplace in the living room watching erotic videos and making love, but I was more interested in sex than in alcohol and paced myself accordingly.

Yet I saw clearly that my drinking would sooner or later come between us if I allowed it to continue. At least once at my schoolhouse apartment I had trouble maintaining an erection with G—— after drinking too many whiskeys before dinner and too much wine. Worse, I began to have attacks of vertigo so intense that when they hit—when I turned over in lovemaking or to get out of bed—the room spun around. I fell sideways if I tried to stand. I assumed that drinking caused the vertigo, a new and more advanced symptom that I feared might signal permanent damage to my middle ear. G—— was frightened for me. I felt like a goddamned fool.

When I put all these pieces together, alone at night in my principal's office under the eaves after a day working on the farm, I saw that they came down to a blunt choice between drinking and having a life. I could probably count on my farmer's tolerance and stumble through the year. I could probably moderate my drinking long enough to allow my middle ear to heal and beat back a health problem for a few years more. The crucial difference was G——. If I kept on drinking, I knew I'd lose her.

That was all I needed to know. I wasn't about to lose G——. She was already the center of my life. I put the bottle away and stopped drinking then and there. I haven't had a drink since, nor even wanted one.

G——'s visits to my country apartment meant that we could spend the night together. We usually made love through the evening on the narrow ledge where I slept, then inflated the larger air mattress and arranged a bed on the floor. Always before with lovers, I had turned away to go to sleep, but I held G—— protectively in my arms. I woke her early in the morning by applying Albolene to her clitoris and stroking her from sleep to flushed, dreamy orgasm; she was still sleepy after she came.

It was wonderful to slide my penis into the hot center of her sleepy body. I'm usually wide-awake as soon as I open my eyes, but I often had trouble climaxing in my turn those early mornings. I'd climb part of the distance and then the sensation would drop off some undefined edge. I think the problem was physiological rather than psychological, although the fact that G—— had to leave to drive back to the city added performance pressure to the mix. Sometimes I huffed and puffed until I hit the dizzy extreme of hyperventilation. Morning was never my favorite time for sex.

One evening when G—— and I were resting from love-making, naked in each other's arms, we heard the entrance doors below us slam. Rowdy voices advanced up the stairs. The next thing we knew, someone was banging on the apartment door. G——'s eyes went wide. I recognized the voices and signaled her to silence—the door was too near in that closet of a room to risk even whispering an explanation. With each pounding fist she flinched. The two teenage sons of the farmer I was working with had decided to pay me an unannounced visit. My room lights were on, my car was parked outside and they couldn't figure out why I didn't answer my door. I prayed I'd locked the son of a bitch. They tormented the doorknob—evidently I had. We could hear them talking. "Why don't he open the door?" "Maybe he's asleep." "Hell, it's too early to be sleepin'. Let's wake him up." They pounded on the door, used a credit card to try to card the latch, pounded on the wall, climbed out over the entrance stairs to try to peek around the edges of the wallpaper that covered the glass interior window. Poor G——. She was rigid in my arms. I don't know how long the assault lasted. It felt like an hour. Finally my galoot friends gave up and clumped away. Then I could explain to G—— who they were. She'd been scared. I had drunken neighbors who sometimes fought in the halls late at night; she'd thought it might be they, coming to get us. We ended up laughing hysterically, picturing the boys' faces if they'd succeeded in forcing the door. They hadn't meant us any harm and I didn't begrudge them the visit. "Where was you last night?" one of them asked me the next morning. "Out jogging," I told him innocently. "Why? Did you come by?" "See," his mother chimed in, "I told you that's where he was." She seemed relieved. But the boys' father avoided my eyes. He was far too canny not to guess why I didn't answer my door that night. He never said a word.

In late autumn I noticed that G——'s nipples had changed. I was surprised that I'd missed the transition; I sucked them often enough. They'd been the nipples of a girl when we first met, hardly different from my own— small bumps that turned white as they erected above diminutive areolas that didn't visibly engorge. Probably because sex stimulated her production of female hormones, they'd become a woman's nipples—browner, larger, fuller, with areolas like caps swelling over the points of her breasts. I'd never heard of such a change in a grown woman before. G—— and I were both amazed. G—— was even a little embarrassed, the way a young woman is sometimes embarrassed by her first pregnancy because it announces to the world that she fucks.

Neither G—— nor I fell instantly in love. Love grew between us, a pattern different for both of us from our previous experiences. I don't remember when I first told G—— I loved her, or when she first told me (she remembers deciding not to be the first to say it—fair enough given the circumstances). Sometime that autumn, possibly around her birthday at the end of October, when I gave her a gold bracelet (she moonlighted with a catering outfit, the only woman among a black-tie crew of gay men; when she demurred from telling them who gave her the gift, they named me "Mr. Bracelet," which was how she introduced me to them later when we met). More clearly I remember when I realized that my relationship with G—— had gone beyond patchwork marital repair. As autumn chilled into winter—bright days on the farm, exhilarating work harvesting under the great blue dome of prairie sky, driving trucks to the elevator piled high with yellow corn—I picked up a copy of a book, *Uncoupling*, that I'd previously browsed in a bookstore and passed over. (How do we know when a book will resonate for us? Choosing the right book is as mysterious as falling in love.) I read *Uncoupling* in one sitting during an evening in the country alone. It drew on extensive interviews to define patterns common to relationships in the process of breaking up. I was shocked to discover that the confusion which I took to be unique was in fact a universal experience. Relationships go up in stages, like buildings being built, and apparently dismantle in stages as well. It's embarrassing to admit that I opened a book and learned there that I would eventually file for divorce, but that's what happened. *Uncoupling* wasn't a crystal ball; it was more like a handbook of diagnostics. I told G—— about it. She said she'd watched other people's relationships break up and the way I'd been talking sounded familiar. I'd been guilty about seeming to string her along, as all her friends (especially her gay friends) warned her married men usually do. She didn't see it that way. She believed me when I said I simply didn't know where I was going yet (but she was glad I'd read the book and found out). She told her friends to back off; she was learning so much from the relationship, she insisted, that she considered it worthwhile even if it came to an early end.

It didn't come to an early end. To the contrary, I understood by midwinter that my marriage, not my affair, was coming to an end. The intense sexuality I'd found with G—— was certainly one reason for making that choice, but it wasn't the only reason—not even the primary reason. The primary reason was so basic it sounds trivial: whether we were naked or clothed, making love or talking, alone together or in company, I felt comfortable with G——. With each of my wives I'd felt a slight but constant anxiety, a sense that they never quite approved of me.

G—— was a wonderful lover, but she was also becoming my best friend. The child in me responded to the child in her—the part we considered our essential identities, the deepest part of ourselves, the part the adults we'd become had fiercely protected—and those two children were so nearly identical in their tastes, their fears, their grave clarity about people and their mischievous and usually bawdy humor that we were frequently astonished by the parallels. As I felt anxious in my marriages, for example, so had G—— felt fearful with the man whom she had loved so intensely before me—afraid, she told me several years later, that he might find out who she "really" was and might not like her, afraid that she couldn't be the kind of person he wanted her to be. G—— felt as comfortable with me as I did with her. For both of us, childhood had been a brutal war; we were like veterans who know they've seen too much to be at ease ever again in their lives with anyone except another veteran. I didn't propose to spend the last third of my life living with anxiety and loneliness. In February I told my wife what was going on. It hurt her very much, and I'm sorry for that. We talked over our problems for several months, and at the beginning of June I moved out.

By then I'd finished my farm research and moved back to the city. I rented an apartment midtown, half a mile from G——'s. We slept at her apartment during the week to keep her cats company and spent weekends at mine.

We pushed our sexual exploration farther that summer. One weekend we spread the bed with a paper drop cloth and a spare sheet and oiled our bodies. Our skin took on the heated lubricity that's usually confined to the genitals in lovemaking; we joined and rejoined, all slippery limbs and hollows, as if we were penises and vulvas both, combined in common orgy.

I was enthralled with G——'s capacity for orgasm. We

experimented with new ways to evoke it. Lying on top of
her, stopped for a rest after peaking myself, I moved my
legs outside hers so that hers closed around my penis. That
brought her clitoris directly into contact with the shaft of
my penis. I began slowly thrusting. She liked the position
and I continued. Very quickly she came to orgasm that way,
her body quivering against me all along its length. I waited
for her brief phase of clitoral hypersensitivity to pass and
began again. She came again, and again. We might have
continued, but with her legs closed her pubic hair abraded
my penis. We moved on to other pleasures.

Closing her legs over my penis became one of
G——'s favorite variations. Once she rested her arms above
her head. Playfully I held them. Afterward she told me
she liked that mild restraint. The next time we lay together
that way I deliberately slipped my hands under her upper
arms and over her forearms, gently levering them down.
As we moved together and her pleasure mounted she
watched me until her eyes fluttered closed and she arched
against me. "I *have* to have orgasm," she described the
fantasy she built on that mild restraint. "You won't let me
go until I do. I feel held in place. Safe." Sometimes, stroking her clitoris with my right hand, I gripped her buttocks
in my left—they were compact enough that one hand could
gather them—another anchoring. "I love it when you hold
me like that," she told me. So restraint, when it's mild and
not coerced, may feel like security rather than punishment.
I'd never thought of it that way before.

In the Marilyn Chambers movie *Insatiable* there's a
scene where an actor playing a gardener roughly seduces
Chambers on a pool table in what is supposed to be her
rich father's game room. At one point she spreads her
shaved labia for him and he pounds his erection against her
clitoris. Since it's meant to be aggressive, a triumph of

crude masculinity over wealth, the riot-stick routine is com-
ical. Once, withdrawing from G—— after a time of peaking, kneeling between her legs with a full, well-oiled
erection, I demonstrated the maneuver for a laugh. To our
mutual surprise G—— found it arousing. I kept up the
pounding, spreading her labia with one hand and wielding
my erection with the other, both of us laughing until excitement set us straight. With her legs splayed G—— had
braced her feet against my thighs; when she came, roaring,
she involuntarily pushed full force and propelled herself
halfway across the bed while I scrambled along on my knees
to catch up.

G—— realized why pounding worked so powerfully for
her one night when her neighbor overhead on the third
floor had a date. The couple fucked three or four times that
night. We nicknamed the date Thumper. He pumped so
hard and fast that he made the bed bang the floor and woke
us up; the cats gathered wide-eyed. We lay awake in the
middle of the summer night giggling and whispering. It
excited us enough to make love again. If G——'s bed had
been spring-loaded like her upstairs neighbor's we might
have started a cascade of copulations down through the
building. G—— connected the noise of the couple upstairs
to her early sexual experiences (after high school—she'd
stayed a virgin until she was eighteen), when the only way
her boyfriends knew to make her come was by hard fucking,
a race like Thumper's between her orgasm and theirs.
Pounding simulated that sensation. Eventually she realized
that if she hooked her feet around my thighs she wouldn't
rocket across the bed.

G——'s comic slang for the vulva was "cookie," one of
her witty sister's coinages. In G——'s experience, men
rarely ate cookie, nor did they know enough to stroke her
clitoris or to use a lubricant. They waited until it was dark,

they drank to get their courage up, they laid on some per-
functory foreplay and then they fucked, and whatever happened for the woman happened within that narrow range—
I've got mine, now you get yours. They didn't even work
to enlarge their own pleasure; once sheathed they drove
more or less straight to ejaculation. Three minutes up and
down: slam, bam, thank you ma'am. I'm not surprised they
had trouble getting it up and keeping it there. G——'s
sample couldn't have been wildly skewed; her experience
seems to be the common lot. It's appalling that men willing
to invest thought and energy in learning a sport or heading
out into the woods to bond with their hairy brothers won't
invest thought and energy in learning how to play gener-
ously at sex. On the evidence, far too many men are sexually
selfish and self-centered, reverting in the intimacy of the
bedroom to mommy's darlings, taking rather than giving,
not required, as girls are required from earliest childhood,
to pay attention to needs other than their own. Women
complain, but bedroom chauvinism is so all-pervasive they
hardly know where to turn.

During the summer G—— decided to quit smoking.
Together we planned a blitzkrieg campaign. Brilliantly, I
think, she decided to drop her weight five pounds below
her ideal *before* she stopped smoking, while she still had
nicotine's boost of appetite suppression, so that the weight
she would probably gain afterward would only bring her
back to where she wanted to be. I recommended she quit
cold turkey over a weekend, doing something to keep busy
and flooding her system with fruit juice. I'd had good luck
walking off the first couple of days of nicotine detox, breathing fresh air. It was too hot that summer for an out-
door strategy to succeed. We decided to substitute sex, a
Labor Day weekend of pleasuring from morning to night,
G——'s choice, ad lib. As she flushed the nicotine from

her system we'd replace it with healing, dreamy endorphins. Fun for her buddy too.

Our weekend of lovemaking worked, though G—— sometimes felt dizzy and disoriented. In my Air Force days I'd monitored patients coming up from anesthesia; I did for her what I did for them, encouraged her to take deep breaths. G——'s sense of proprioception went screwy as well; she bumped into tables and walked into doors.

Going back to the radio station on Monday was the hardest part. She did fine until Thursday night, when she arrived at my apartment after her show in a state of panicky paranoia, convinced she was going crazy. The attack passed. Fortunately she could sleep.

G—— quit smoking permanently the first time she tried. She was a disciplined woman. She moved on in karate as well. She arrived at my apartment one summer Saturday completely exhausted from pumping four hundred pushups that morning. Her notebook of *katas* was thicker, and before the summer was over she tested for her purple belt. I did three hours of low-impact aerobics a week—I was twice the age of anyone else in the class—and I could manage thirty pushups on a good day. I wasn't ashamed of my condition, but I didn't ask G—— to wrestle.

She disliked her overbite. She wanted to have her teeth straightened but couldn't afford the work. I'd been through braces with my son and knew what a long haul they were. I considered giving G—— braces for Christmas. That would be a long-term commitment, and I'd had bad luck with long-term commitments; I didn't want this one to go the way the others had gone. Then I realized I was corrupting the gift by tying it to a commitment, mine or G——'s. Whether the relationship lasted or not, wasn't a gift a gift? Or did I mean to cut off payments if G—— and I split? One other cavil nagged me: I liked G——'s overbite. Would I like her looks as much without it? Embarrassing, but there it was. Slap that man up the side of the head. Was I giving a gift or trying to play Pygmalion? If G—— wanted her teeth straightened, what better Christmas present?

I called the orthodontist her dentist had recommended, asked his secretary to send me one of his business cards and glued it inside a Christmas card ("There IS a Santa Claus"). G—— was overwhelmed. Then it was her turn to worry about the commitment the gift seemed to imply; I had to convince her to accept it. It was important to her. Her parents had neglected her teeth so badly when she was a child that she'd had serious periodontal problems as a young adult. Offering to finance her orthodontics was offering to compensate for that neglect. As I intended and as she immediately realized, it was another way to tell her that I loved her and wished her well. I did. So we held each other that Christmas morning, and wept together and knew joy.

She went to see the orthodontist, a young man starting a new practice, a Mayo man. He took the usual X rays and measurements and molds. A week later we both sat in his office waiting to hear what course of treatment he'd recommend. Then it was my turn to be overwhelmed. He recommended G—— undergo surgery to lengthen her lower jaw. She'd still need two years of braces first, but the surgery would reduce her time in braces by as much as three years. More to the point, it was the proper treatment for her particular condition. It happened to cost three times as much. A gift is a gift. I swallowed hard and said yes.

G—— got her braces, porcelain brackets glued onto the outside surface of her teeth rather than old-fashioned metal bands. She had to wax them at first to keep them from lacerating the inside of her mouth. They made her lips protrude, which changed the feel but not the fun of kissing.

Both of us worried about the damage her appliances might do to fellatio. Patiently for a year G—— had coaxed me to believe she enjoyed taking my penis into her mouth and licking and drafting me to orgasm. She grew better and better at it as the year went on; I grew more and more relaxed. It came to be my preferred mode of ejaculatory orgasm after I'd extended first-stage orgasm through our hours of sexual play: G—— licking and drafting and sucking me, twisting her small hand or her warm mouth around my glans, her other hand working my scrotum, until I bucked and pounded the bed and came in multiple pulses with a sustained, open-throated shout. She always swallowed my gush of semen; I could smell it musky on her breath when she slipped up beside me afterward to cuddle, looking shy and pleased. She swore she liked the taste. (I liked the idea: my penis conflated with the breast, nursing her as I'd dreamed once of nursing myself.) I showed her an erotic video of a woman deep-throating and she quickly picked up the technique. When she'd first begun fellating me she'd knelt on the bed at right angles to my body. I moved her around so that she knelt alongside me with her buttocks beside my face, where I could hold her small hips, watch her breasts swing and play with her vulva—warm and wet by then and slick with lubricant—while she drafted. The orgasm she gave me with her mouth was far and away the most powerful ecstasy I had ever felt. G—— liked doing it and I liked having it done, so much so that we ended almost every session of lovemaking that way. I went for weeks without ejaculating in her vagina, though I certainly spent enough time there. We joked that she didn't really need birth control.

Braces, we were relieved to discover, didn't interfere with oral sex.

I'd wanted to move out of the Midwest for at least the past ten years. I'd lived there most of my life and raised my children there; I was ready for a change. I considered northern California, but the center of my business was New York. I decided to move to the East Coast, and not long after Christmas I asked G—— to move with me.

Moving was a wrenching decision for G——. Unlike mine, her work wasn't portable. Moving with me would mean that for a time at least she'd have to accept my support, which roused her worst insecurities. She wanted a fresh start as much as I did, but given her childhood she was understandably wary of becoming dependent. Even after she agreed to go with me she discovered new reservations. I had to work to resist resenting her skepticism, to believe that it concerned her past more than her present. I pointed out that selling her car and the contents of her apartment would leave her with several thousand dollars in the bank, enough to walk out if she ever felt she had to. During the ensuing weeks of anxious and sometimes angry discussion I realized that the least hint, ever, that I thought I was buying her, or owned her, or that she was less than an equal partner because we'd be living for a time off the money I earned, would certainly drive her away. It's unusual in a relationship to know so clearly what act must be irrevocably destructive, and the following fall, when G—— and I went through a rocky period, I sometimes felt as if I were walking around with a loaded gun in my belt. It didn't go off because I'd worked the problem through even before I invited G—— to move. I had resources that G—— didn't have (not surprising, since my career was twenty years farther along) that I proposed to share with her. I wanted to share what I had because I loved her, but sharing was in any case a fair exchange, a quid pro quo, because I was asking her to make a major sacrifice on my behalf, to give over secure work for an uncertain market in Boston or New York.

Fortunately G—— agreed. Early the following summer, having sold everything we owned except my small car and our books and clothes, with the two cats in airline boxes in the back seat and a jammed U-Haul trailer pitching behind like a sea anchor, G—— and I moved together to the East Coast to start a new life. I was then fifty-one; she was thirty-three.

Adjustment was harder than we expected. We'd chosen to settle at least provisionally in an academic community and neither one of us felt at home there. G—— knew no one. That was the rocky time. We took our insecurities out on each other—hours and days of smoldering resentment, flashing anger, barely checked rage. G—— turned brittle and defensive when we fought. I turned cold. Our fighting that fall almost broke us up. G—— started a long course of psychotherapy. But always, without exception, when we traced a conflict back to its point of origin, we discovered that it started with a literal misunderstanding, a statement or a tone of voice misunderstood that others had used in the past to hurt us. Then we rediscovered gratefully that we really did wish each other well.

Living together, both of us working at home, our lovemaking settled into regularity. The Brauers recommend that couples appoint times for lovemaking, at least three trysts a week, preferably not at bedtime (G—— and I hadn't made love at bedtime, except for what we called snaps—quickies—for more than a year). We set aside two-hour periods on Thursday, Saturday and Sunday afternoons. New friends came calling during those hours at first, especially on the weekends, following the community's old-fashioned traditions. Rather than greet them in our bathrobes we countered with another old-fashioned tradition and pretended we weren't home. We'd rented a drafty old three-story house on a quiet residential side street, and now that we knew our neighbors, we had to deal with the noise we made making love. We closed the bedroom windows, but it was evident from the way distinguished full professors passing us on the street found themselves unable to meet our eyes that some of our hallelujahs got through.

Winter clamped down in that cold northern city. We moved a space heater into the bedroom and played. G——'s orgasmic capacity entranced me more than ever. With my mouth, with my hands, with my penis, I licked and stroked and pounded her to multiple orgasms, as many as fourteen in one afternoon.

We hadn't tried to extend her orgasm. ESO required alternating internal vaginal stimulation on the upper vaginal wall with clitoral stimulation, and G——'s bladder irritability, which she was now treating with medication, made the internal stimulation uncomfortable. But G——'s multiple orgasm blended over. One sign the Brauers had observed of extended orgasmic response in women was what they called "push-outs"—the woman bearing down as women do during labor to increase her level of excitement, relaxing and pushing out her vaginal and anal sphincters rather than tightening them. As G—— approached her most intense orgasms, well along in our afternoons of lovemaking, I noticed that her labia and her anus pushed out. She'd found the technique on her own and used it to intensify her pleasure.

By spring we were happier. I'd finished the farm book and started writing a memoir of my childhood. G—— was interviewing people for a book of her own. We'd been through her surgery by then and she had a stronger chin and a fine new bite. But a subtle change had come into our lovemaking, a change that disturbed and worried me: though we still found time for long afternoons together, G—— seemed to have trouble multiplying her orgasms past the first two or three. I thought I'd lost my touch. Then I began to sense resistance when I tried to push her to more orgasms. I put off asking her about it; I was afraid of what she'd say.

Our landlord wanted his house back for the summer. For the rent we were paying in that upscale market we could afford to summer anywhere in the world. I knew I'd be writing the darkest part of my childhood book during the summer. I wanted to find a sun-filled place where it was warm, to counteract the terrible darkness and cold I remembered from the two late-childhood years when I was dirty, ragged, semi-homeless and starved. We'd have to take the cats. G—— made a foray to St. Croix to scout a place and found a Hollywood house of glass and marble with a swimming pool at the height of a hill. We flew there in June on separate flights, one cat per cabin, all the airline allowed.

We learned to scuba dive that summer, both of us overcoming serious inland phobias of drowning in the sea. The cats ran from room to room at night trying to escape the cloud-mist that blew through the open-louvered house. We brought along a bag of books we'd always wanted to read— in my case the *Satyricon*, Heraclitus, *Tristram Shandy*. I wrote the middle of my childhood book, shaken by the helplessness I had to relive. It was painful to reexperience the suffering of the eleven-year-old child I had been, to admit the losses that for more than thirty years I had shrugged off stoically or denied. Looking up from my laptop in late morning was like waking from a nightmare; I was astonished to see the green island falling away from the open house to the cobalt sea, astonished that the sunlight washed the air.

We spent part of each afternoon sunning naked beside the pool. The pool boy popped up too often and randomly for us to make love outside. But a hilltop breeze always blew through the big master bedroom and the bed was canopied with gauze.

We had brought along a manuscript copy of a second Brauer book I had helped Alan and Donna write during the previous summer and fall, a sequel to *ESO* called *The ESO Ecstasy Program* that enlarged on the first book's information and organized it far more formally into a series of exercises. We proposed to test it to see if it worked and to explore the unacknowledged impasse we had come to.

The first week of the program called for meditation and sex-muscle exercises, for kissing practice and massage and communication. Initially it went well, I wrote in the file of notes I was keeping:

We sunned another hour beside the pool and practiced snorkeling. Then we showered for ESO training, the "sensual focus massage with verbal feedback." While we readied for massage the rain swept up the hill and over the house, a downpour that we hope refilled the house cistern, rich smell of wet soil and bush. Peaceful twenty minutes in turn enjoying a rubdown with lotion, a short break, then lovemaking: G—— to orgasm once with my mouth, her legs around my head, then again with my penis with her legs closed inside mine. She's lovely in her new tan, seamless from top to toe: even her labia are tanning, and her pubic hair bleaching blond. Then she rode me to multiple peaks and took me in her mouth; I thrashed in convulsion, nailed to the bed.

But very quickly the communication structure that the Brauers' program imposed broke down. The disagreement that G—— and I had come to was beyond its capacity to contain.

I complained that she seemed to be retreating from lovemaking. She took a deep breath, looked me in the eye and told me bluntly that she felt pushed. She didn't want so many orgasms, she said. She'd come to dread them, dread the pressure to have them. She was afraid she'd eventually dread making love. She loved making love with me, she didn't want to disappoint me, but having orgasm after orgasm wasn't what she liked.

I asked her what she liked. She said she liked being free to choose how many orgasms she would have. I asked her how many she thought she'd choose. She said she'd probably choose one or two.

I've never been angrier in my life. I felt so much rage at that moment, so much hatred, that I couldn't even talk. I wanted to smash G——. I wanted to walk out. A black wind of the purest paranoia chilled me to the bone. We had come so far together, we had committed so much, put down so many roots, organized so interconnected a life, yet abruptly I was visited with the dogmatic, paranoid conviction that G—— had exercised her remarkable sexuality over the past two years as a setup, purely to con me, and having arrived in the midst of the life we led, was now springing the trap.

I told her so. She was shocked and hurt that I had so completely misunderstood her.

We discussed it, argued about it, fought over it for the next four days. Otherwise we hardly spoke. I felt particularly betrayed that she had waited until we'd moved all the way to St. Croix, until the beginning of what was supposed to be an idyllic, productive summer, to drop her bomb—as if we hadn't agreed to wait to talk everything over in the context of the Brauer program, as if I hadn't also saved up my concerns. I fantasized what I was certain had to follow: leaving, separating, living alone, finding someone else. I fantasized whom I might find. For once fantasy was tiresome. One orgasm or ten, I'd never been happier with anyone than I'd been with G——.

Slowly my rage abated and I began to be able to hear what G—— was saying. She was saying that she loved me, that she wanted to be with me, but that her body was her own, that her ecstasy was her own, that she could share it but not license it out. She was risking everything (but my obsession had put everything at risk) to persuade me that she wasn't an erotic fantasy but a woman in my arms.

I didn't understand why she'd changed. She'd seemed to enjoy multiple orgasm earlier in the relationship. But she hadn't changed, she told me. She'd begun to feel pressured when we'd started living together, before we moved east. When we saw each other only once a week her urgency was naturally higher. When we made love three or four times a week for an hour or more each time, that same urgency distributed across the more frequent meetings. She'd had eight or ten orgasms with me when we made love once a week. She wanted to continue having about that many when we made love three times a week. My obsession with her performance had pressured her to triple that frequency. It was more than she could bear. She'd been afraid to tell me, afraid that she'd lose me.

I saw finally that from whatever point of innocence we'd begun, I'd evolved to something like a vampire. A young woman drunk with sensation, overstimulated, perpetually orgasmic, was the ecstatic figure illuminated at the center of my microdot. There was nothing wrong with linking that eroticized revision of my childhood torture to G——'s unusual sexual capacity so long as she was a willing volunteer. But pressuring her to reenact my fantasy, as I had unwittingly done, tortured her. Stimulating her to orgasm after orgasm was like tickling a child and refusing to stop. And that made me her torturer, an apprentice to the stepmother whose cruelty still haunted me.

I gave up my obsession reluctantly. Across the remainder of a wonderful summer G—— and I found our way back together. It helped to work through the program exercises. We taught each other new pleasures, delicacies we'd overlooked. I stopped trying to control my sensation and let G—— take charge when she pleasured me. I paid more attention to receiving pleasure and gave it less relentlessly. That brought our exchange back into balance. Sometimes I missed G——'s starburst of orgasms. Sometimes I still do.

You can't have *all*. *All* is for dictators and divinities; *all* is terror and laying waste. Not *all* but *enough*, writes Leonard Shengold. G—— and I find enough together, a harvest of enough, a bounty. We love each other, we help each other, we wake in the morning happy to be together. Is there anything on this earth finer than two human beings turned to each other in a comfortable bed, one's leg thrown over the other's hip, looking into each other's eyes, sharing the dawning day? It's the very root and core of human freedom: the little democracy of the bedroom.

We make love less often than we used to. We tell each other that's because our lives are so full. Our lovemaking's more stylized, less experimental. We know exactly how to please each other and do it well. From impassioned sexuality we've moved to a less frenzied intimacy—emotionally as well as sexually—that feels like what we assume "normal" must be. Our childhoods didn't prepare us for normalcy; to us it's mysterious and exotic. We're surprised to discover we like it. Within its security, intimacy opens out into a great sunlit space of happiness. Dark passages still extend away. Light can never reach them all.

We haven't married. When friends ask us why not we say we don't want to ruin a good relationship. We've become each other's guardians, fiercely protective. Our disagreements still invariably trace back to misunderstandings, to apprehensions left over from childhood. We're best friends. Though we only refer to the future obliquely, we're preparing to grow old together.

I still catch my breath at the delicacy of G——'s shoulders, so strong and so brave, so small.

And so, in the words of Ernst Jünger's old-fashioned Captain Richard, "Here is our kingdom, the best of monarchies, the best republic. Here is our garden, our happiness." We received it as a gift, for better and for worse, as all life comes.

Glade
1991

Freight

Claire Hurt Bishop and Kurt Wiese, *The Five Chinese Brothers*. Coward-McCann, 1938.

Alan and Donna Brauer, *ESO*. Warner, 1983.

———, *The ESO Ecstasy Program*. Warner, 1990.

Alex Comfort, *The Joy of Sex*. Crown, 1972.

Seymour Fisher, *The Female Orgasm*. Basic Books, 1973.

Ernst Jünger, *The Glass Bees*. Noonday Press, 1960.

Claude Lévi-Strauss, *The Savage Mind*. University of Chicago Press, 1966.

Joyce Carol Oates, *On Boxing*. Doubleday, 1987.

Wardell Pomeroy, *Dr. Kinsey and the Institute for Sex Research.* Yale University Press, 1972.

John Richardson, *A Life of Picasso.* Random House, 1991.

Leonard Shengold, *Soul Murder.* Yale University Press, 1989.

————, *Father, Don't You See I'm Burning?* Yale University Press, 1991.

Robert Stoller, *Sexual Excitement.* Pantheon, 1979.

Gay Talese, *Thy Neighbor's Wife.* Doubleday, 1980.

Robert Thom, *Children of the Ladybug.* Yale University Press, 1956.

George E. Vaillant, *The Natural History of Alcoholism.* Harvard University Press, 1983.

Diane Vaughan, *Uncoupling.* Vintage, 1986.

William Butler Yeats, "Brown Penny," *Collected Poems.* Macmillan, 1951.